Praise for **Fierce and Delicate**

"Many dancers wrestle with one of the central questions of Renée Nicholson's fabulous book: How does one live as an ex-dancer? The answers Nicholson explores will strongly resonate with those who long to lift the veil that shrouds creative pursuits in unnecessary mystique. I love Nicholson's powerful prose: how the essays circle in and out of dance, the way movement comes alive on the page, and the articulate grace with which Nicholson writes about sudden disability. In *Fierce and Delicate*, Nicholson teaches us how to envelop our impossible dreams with gratitude for the life we have now."

—Renée E. D'Aoust, author of *Body of a Dancer*

"Renée Nicholson writes with the grace, determination, and, yes, fierceness needed to succeed in the world of professional dance, so it is no surprise that *Fierce and Delicate* is such a remarkable and *en pointe* memoir-in-essays, as breathtaking and beautiful as ballet itself. Nicholson's voice blends absolute honesty with a lovely, lyrical descriptive style, and each essay is a pure pleasure to read. Bravo!"

—Dinty W. Moore, author of *Between Panic and Desire*

Fierce and Delicate

Essays on Dance and Illness

RENÉE K. NICHOLSON

West Virginia University Press · Morgantown

Copyright © 2021 by West Virginia University Press
All rights reserved
First edition published 2021 by West Virginia University Press
Printed in the United States of America

ISBN 978-1-952271-01-4 (paperback) / ISBN 978-1-952271-02-1
(ebook)

Library of Congress Cataloging-in-Publication Data
Names: Nicholson, Renée K., author.
Title: Fierce and delicate : essays on dance and illness / Renée K.
    Nicholson.
Description: First edition. | Morgantown : West Virginia University Press,
    2021. | Includes bibliographical references.
Identifiers: LCCN 2020051735 | ISBN 9781952271014 (paperback) |
    ISBN 9781952271021 (ebook)
Subjects: LCSH: Nicholson, Renée K. | Ballet dancers—United States—
    Biography. | Rheumatoid arthritis—Patients—United States—Biog-
    raphy.
Classification: LCC GV1785.N487 A3 2021 | DDC 792.802/8092 [B]—
    dc23
LC record available at https://lccn.loc.gov/2020051735

Book and cover design by Than Saffel / WVU Press
Cover photograph by bezikus / Shutterstock

Essays in this collection previously appeared in the following publica-
tions: "When I Was a Mouse" in *Prime Number* 11, no. 3 (2012); "Five
Positions" in *The Gettysburg Review* 20, no. 3 (2007) and in *Redux*;
"Never Famous" in *Stymie*; "Raked Stages: A Twelve-Step Program" in
Perigee: A Journal of the Arts; "Coda: Partnering" in *Blue Lyra Review* 3
(2013); "Out of the Blue" in *Cleaver Magazine* 1 (2013); "Hair: A Short
History" in *Switchback* 16, no. 8 (2012); "In Sickness" in *Moon City
Review* (2013); "A Royal in Appalachia" in *Barely South Review* (2014);
"Certified" in *Midwestern Gothic* 19 (2015); selections from "Fierce and
Delicate," published under the title "Standing Tall," in *Crosstimbers*; and
"Six Impossible Things Before Breakfast" in *Typehouse Magazine* 6, no.
2, issue 17 (2019).

For my parents, who helped me become a dancer, and for Dominique, who reminds me of my love for ballet.

Contents

Part I

A Girl Who Wanted to Fly

When I Was a Mouse

THE YEAR THE SINK FELL in our dressing room, I was the littlest mouse. When the sink fell, water sprayed out into the long room. The sink had been attached to a wall with no pedestal or cabinet underneath for support. Just an old sink with rust stains around the drain. The wall was painted gray, fluorescent lights shone overhead, and mirrors lined the opposite wall. When the sink fell, no one touched it, although the backstage moms in charge of our dressing room had told us to wash our hands.

Instead, we gathered our bags and costumes and marched out—me petrified that I'd be blamed for the sink, because it hadn't occurred to me that the theater's backstage was old and maintenance shoddy, because I had complained out loud about the pink canvas shoes we had to wear with our costumes. I figured I was already branded a troublemaker and the fallen sink would be blamed on me. I was sure of it.

I preferred leather shoes to canvas. Party scene children wore black leather slippers.

Damp and cramped in the hallway, the legion of little mice was quickly divided. All the mice were small; the taller girls our age were soldiers. Many were nice. We rehearsed with them every weekend in Studio B until we moved into the theater. Unlucky me, not sent to the soldiers' dressing room.

In the Party Girls' dressing room, the dancers kept their hair gelled around foam curlers so that onstage they all had perfect ringlets. Costumes with petticoats and ribbons, too. The Party Girls smeared crimson over their lips, their backstage mothers coating girlish lashes with mascara. Many begged for false eyelashes, like the ones the company women wore. Chatter was high-pitched and pointed. The Party Girls did not like mice, even though most mice, like me, were also angels in act 2.

"I have been in the party scene for two years," a red-headed Party Girl said. "I only did battle scene my first year."

"Stay still," a backstage mom said, and then swiped a huge blush brush over her daughter's cheek.

The girl's friend, a little blond with a head full of pink foam curlers nodded. She waited for her blush and then said, "I'm the youngest of the party scene girls."

"How old?" redhead asked.

"Eleven," curler-head replied.

When I was a mouse, I thought as a mouse. I crept around the outskirts of their conversation. Paid attention, looked for cheese and mischief.

"Last year there was a ten-year-old girl in party scene," the redhead said.

"Most ten-year-olds are still in Battle," the curler-head said.

I smoothed my hands along my pink tights, fresh from the Capezio wrapper. My mother bought them especially for performing. No holes or runs. The Party Girls narrowed their eyes, heavy with mascara and eye shadow. I didn't need makeup because I wore a mouse head. My face would be done when I morphed into angel.

Curler-head pointed a slim finger at me. "How old are you?"

"In ten days I'll be eight," I said.

"That's too young," redhead said, her voice raising an octave so that she nearly squealed it. I'd made her mad.

"I don't believe you," curler-head said. She stared down her own reflection in the big lighted mirror on the wall of the Party Girls' dressing room. Another mouse told her it was true. We were supposed to get a cake the night of my birthday, to have after the performance. We performed until Christmas Eve, my birthday only a few days before.

Many years later, in Studio Nine at American Ballet Theatre, I would be told, half joking, that little girls are evil, that anyone working with children should read *The Lord of the Flies*.

"They make you wear a mouse head because you are ugly and need to hide your face," curler-head said. She kept staring at herself in the mirror, fussing with a foam curler near her cheek. "Only the prettiest girls get party scene. One of us will surely be Clara soon."

"You might never get in party scene," redhead said. "Or you might have to play a boy." Sometimes girls would have to play boys in the party scene because there were never enough boys for the parts. Mice and soldiers were better than that fate.

"Everyone knows mice aren't good dancers," said another Party Girl, wanting in.

I looked down at my feet, covered by the wretched canvas shoes. The girls were laughing at me. "You don't even get a good dressing room," curler-head said. "Even your stupid sink doesn't like you."

I wanted to cry but didn't. I wanted to take off those canvas shoes and hurl them at the Party Girls. Instead, I fiddled with the elastics, trying to come up with a real good reply, one that would shut them up. My ears filled with the sound of my own blood pumping. Then I heard my name.

"Quick!" said the director of the children. She was a dark-haired woman with slim arms and legs and a long, imperial nose. "We need you for a photo shoot with the Company Mice."

I heard the chorus of Party Girls. The words *photo* and *shoot* being repeated, slowly, up and down, a complaint. There were little mice like me and big mice, men from the company, and the Mouse King, also from the company. The paper wanted mice pictures. The paper wanted the little mouse. Me. I could have stuck my tongue out at those Party Girls. But I didn't.

Within a week, the wall was patched where the sink fell, and the mice got a dressing room again. Over the place where there used to be a sink, my friends taped a copy of the newspaper picture of me and the big mice. They wrote happy birthday and signed their names. They asked the big mice to sign and they did, and on my birthday the little mice and big mice and even some of the soldiers and third act gingersnaps sang to me, and I wished hard and blew out all the candles in one breath.

Five Positions

Once burned by milk you will blow on cold water.

—Russian Proverb

WHILE I WAS A DANCER, I collected quotes from famous people in the dance world and from the less famous Russians I met in ballet. Because Russia produced so many proficient dancers, they completely infiltrated my American experience, the influence of their methodology everywhere. They often shared with me their proverbs, sayings meant to convey their truth, but perhaps veiled, as I often veil my own. Their proverbs, like their technique, went straight to the heart of things. But the proverbs were difficult and, like ballet steps, could never fully be mastered.

George Balanchine Americanized ballet, but he was originally trained in St. Petersburg. Like the other Russians, Balanchine was famous for his proverbs, most of which he concocted; he was also famous for his ballerinas: very young, very thin, a blend of athlete and siren. He invented the baby ballerina. If old Hollywood immortalized the sexy, curvy blond, Balanchine created a new fetish: the sleek brunette. Of course, when I was seven and first stepped into a proper ballet class, I had no idea about any of this.

FIRST

A Russian proverb: you do not need a whip to urge on an obedient horse. In the first year of ballet training, we learned to bend, plié, and to stretch the leg and the foot, tendu; then we learned to sketch circles with our pointed foot on the floor, rond de jambe par terre. "Pull your stomach in," instructed Ms. Helen, my first teacher. "Derrière tucked under. Turn out from the hips. Lead with the heel of your foot." Holding my stomach in was the hardest part.

"In first position," said Ms. Helen, "make a slice of pie with your feet. Stand with heels together, legs and feet turned out, pointing away from the body. Turn out from the hips as much as possible, and do not let your knees or ankles twist." I tied my hair back into a bun, little sprigs defiant at the temples. I wore pink tights, forest green leotard with cap sleeves, little pink Capezio slippers, soft leather, elastics sewn at the heel.

Made up in thick blue eyeliner and dark mauve lipstick, Ms. Helen kept her hair short. She wore chiffon skirts in pink and jeweled green. She wore clogs and smelled of heavy perfume. I thought she was glamorous.

My first pair of slippers: "You have to fit them tightly," said the woman at the dance store. "The teachers won't like it unless they're snug. Ballet is not something you can grow into." The sales lady had a mass of carrot red hair on top of her head in a messy knot. With her stubby fingers, she checked the fit of the slippers.

Ms. Helen told us to open our legs into a straddle split. Mine: straight out to each side—splat!—open! After that class, Ms. Helen talked to my mom, and I started taking classes twice a week. By the time I was ten, I took ballet every day.

I liked the end of the barre work, when we did the high kicks called grands battements. My leg flew into the air: front, then side, back, and side, turned out from the hip, presented up with a swoosh. A perfectly pointed foot. Sometimes, I felt like a little pixie as I performed a combination with frappés, the fast strikes of the foot that begin at the ankle. After the barre and before the adagio, we stretched. I had no patience for adagio, for those slow, controlled movements. I wanted to jump and spin.

Mom picked me up from school in her cream Tercel station wagon. She listened to the oldies station as she drove me to the ballet studios. My ballet bag was already in the car. Once she dropped me off, I darted inside. I had to get ready for class quickly; if we weren't ready for class—leotard and tights and shoes on and hair neatly pulled into a bun—the teachers wouldn't let us take the class. I couldn't be late. I couldn't be sloppy. I couldn't miss class.

I learned to make a bun all by myself. I pulled my hair into a sleek ponytail, braided it, and looped it into a little knot, securing it with a few bobby pins. I wrapped a hair net around it, securing that with more bobby pins: some the regular flat kind, others U-shaped. I shook my head from side to side to make sure it would stay put. I had my own hairspray, which I kept in my ballet bag, using two or three squirts to hold the hair in place or to smooth little strands near my temples.

In the hallways, I saw the older girls in their cut-up sweatshirts, leg warmers, and plastic pants, torsos folded over their own legs. One girl held another girl's ankles as she lay flat on the floor. Then, she arched her back up, counted to twenty, holding position. Already I wanted the plastic pants and pink leg warmers of the older girls. They looked exotic; they wore lipstick and mascara. I became aware of their beauty.

Gelsey Kirkland, one of Balanchine's baby ballerinas who would go on to dance with Baryshnikov, was an angel in *The Nutcracker* at age nine. It was her first role on stage, just like me (although I was also a mouse that year). She writes, "I was no more than eleven when my mother found me sleepwalking in the middle of the night with my ballet bag in hand."

SECOND

A Russian proverb: if you are afraid of the wolf, don't go into the forest. In ballet, there was always an awareness of other dancers. I wrote the names of other ballet students in my diary. Tameka, who was very tall for her age. Ashley, who had a snub nose. I wonder if they wrote about me:

Renée, who had freckles, but who could jump.

Renée, who has already been an angel, a gingersnap, and a mouse. Who would be in the party scene.

Our progress was often gauged by those early roles, my first awareness of the competitiveness of ballet dancers. Or maybe it was the older girls stretching in the halls.

I skipped through the steps of the petit allegro: sauté, royale, changement; the key to these little jumps was to hold your stomach in. Use a deep plié, bend the knees, and release. In my diary I wrote the names of the steps. I wrote about other things, too. I began to wonder if I would grow up to be pretty. And when would I begin to work in pointe shoes, sur la pointe?

On Saturdays I didn't have class. In the fall there would be class because of *The Nutcracker* rehearsals, but it was just a warm-up; it wasn't meant to improve or teach technique. Usually on Saturdays I had ice cream with my dad. We both loved chocolate in waffle cones.

When did I hear about the dancer at the Bolshoi Ballet who was fired because she ate ice cream? It didn't matter that she weighed only 110 pounds. They fired her. She was a prima ballerina, though, and her audience loved her. So the Bolshoi hired her back.

Not all dancers are that lucky.

By fourteen, I was spending my summers away from home to train. To go to Interlochen Arts Academy, I had to audition to be accepted. Once there, I auditioned again and was placed into a division based on my skills. A summer at Interlochen—just like a summer at any company school— can make or break a ballet student. Some will go home and train harder; others will train at the academy for the school year. Some will quit ballet and never look back.

There were students in visual arts, choir, writing, orchestra, and dance. Hundreds of artistic kids in one place. It was sort of like school, but everyone was talented, focused. There was competitiveness in the air: who was best in what? Everyone was aware of who was best, who was up-and-coming, who had a long way to go. In the cafeteria, the dancers only picked from the salad bar. We all wore uniforms, but the dancers, with our skinny legs poking out from the navy Bermuda shorts, hair up in buns, were easy to spot.

In these years, I idolized Suzanne Farrell of the New York City Ballet. She was first among Balanchine's muses. He loved her for her off-balance balances. Before Balanchine, she was Susie Fricker of Cincinnati, Ohio. He remade her. He said, "First comes the sweat. Then comes the beauty if you're very lucky and have said your prayers."

THIRD

A Russian proverb: don't blame the mirror if your face is crooked. Most girls go through an awkward stage, caught between the little girl and the young woman. But I was caught between a little girl and a young ballerina. Yet by fourteen, I could do nearly anything in pointe shoes that I could do in my soft shoes. The benefit of being a quick study with strong ankles. I perfected a technique for preparing my toes, using thick white medical tape to ward off blisters. The soft shoes didn't get much use.

When I came home from Interlochen Arts Academy, my teachers noticed my improvement. Mrs. Gooden made a list of places I should audition for the following summer. Mr. Franklin said, "Try a little mascara. Some blush and lipstick, too."

Ms. Leigh invited me to take her class but said, "You have to continue to work, to work *very hard*." Ms. Leigh was over fifty, still lean, but with sharp features wrinkled from chain smoking. She knew hard work. She had once been a soloist with the National Ballet of Canada until her Achilles tendon snapped and rolled up her leg like a window shade.

My favorite part of class was the petit allegro, although I also enjoyed the big leaps, the grand allegro. I knew what it meant to soar, even just for a few seconds. I had what the men were taught to cultivate: ballon, or suspension in the air while leaping. Sometimes I took the men's class just to jump. I liked to bounce; I actually allowed myself to have fun. The connecting steps and the big leap performed diagonally across the floor: tombé, pas de bourée, glissade, grand jété. If you say them right, even the words sound jaunty.

Mr. Franklin said it wouldn't hurt to pay attention to my diet. I stopped eating ice cream with my dad. I got a scale for my bathroom, checked my weight daily. I took classes on Saturdays now, and I hated Sundays because there wasn't any ballet. I began to learn the classic variations: Finger Fairy and Bluebird from *The Sleeping Beauty*, and the solo from the third act of *Don Quixote*—the one that's performed only in Russia. My muscle memory became bits and pieces of the classic repertoire.

With birthday money, I bought a pair of plastic pants to warm up in. They made me sweat. I thought of the weight I might lose. But when I looked in the mirror, I hated myself. And mirrors were everywhere. I couldn't stop looking, even if I wanted to. Balanchine said, "The mirror is not you. The mirror is you looking at yourself."

During my summer at the prestigious ballet school, I was chosen to do the Bluebird variation and pas de deux in the summer showcase. My dormitory suitemates weren't chosen to solo. They were dressed in white tulle, on stage among many others dressed in white tulle. Up close, the costumes were smudged and dirty and smelled of sweat.

I told them, "It's important to learn to dance in the corps if you want to get into a ballet company." They had teased me, and it was my turn with the knife. It was a tactic. I hoped to isolate myself from them. Every ballet dancer has her own brand of bitch that she uses to protect herself. Mine was to remove myself from those around me. I was remote and cultivated superior airs: *don't talk to me; don't waste my time.* I was competitive in a way that made friendships nearly impossible. But I was also very lonely. During my ballet years, I don't think anyone knew my favorite color was aqua. They never asked, and I never told. Ballet wasn't about being personal.

My partner in the Bluebird variation and pas de deux was Joe, an athletic dancer two years older than me. He was black and wondered if that would hold him back in ballet. "In ballet," he said, "if you're black, everyone wants you to be the next Arthur Mitchell." In 1955 Mitchell had joined Balanchine's New York City Ballet. Joe said, "The myth was that because you were black that you could not do classical dance." I reminded him that as a male, he would be coveted by many companies; there were never enough male dancers. Joe was kind to me. Sometimes we shared a Diet Coke before our rehearsal. He was in love with another dancer at the company school. Karina. She was lovely: creamy pale skin and light blue eyes and the lightest blond hair, so light that on stage she looked almost bald. Karina was performing another solo in the summer showcase. She had a lovely sense of line when she danced, as if her body was meant to be in arabesque. There was something so natural about it. I watched her, but I also watched Joe watching her. He was reverent in his admiration; it was what I wanted someday. It was how I thought a man should look at a woman.

We were rehearsed by a middle-aged Russian dancer retired from performing. When I first met her, she said, "Your cheeks look so round. You have face like pumpkin." Her advice? Eat less. "Face will lose the baby fat, you see. You like little girl, but you are not anymore."

In the Bluebird variation I did échappés, springing up sur la pointe in fourth, snapping back to fifth, then out to second position. Sometimes I felt exposed. On stage I was no longer just an insecure ballet student. I heard the music of my variation, and my muscles took over. The only thing that mattered was the dancing. The first time in Bluebird, I was made up in heavy eyeliner and pancake makeup. The lights were hot, and the audience was one big shadow. On stage, I searched for myself through the execution of steps. One of the greatest ballet dancers of all time was Margot Fonteyn. She said, "Great artists are people who find ways to be themselves in their art." The Russian who rehearsed us said the clumsy dancer blames her skirt.

FOURTH

A Russian proverb: don't make me kiss, and you will not make me sin. Partnering classes, where the boys and girls learn to dance pas de deux, were tough for me because I was uncomfortable being touched by boys. I had the tiny buds of breasts. My freckles were fading; my skin was very pale. Sometimes I broke out, even though I scrubbed every night, determined not to be plagued by acne. It came anyway, angry. The boys with their hands at my waist, under my thigh, or pressed at the small of my back. I always blushed.

I had my first kiss at one of the lakes around Interlochen Arts Academy, with a trumpet player named Mike. He had dark hair and, of course, strong lips. I thought maybe his lips were strong from trumpet practice, but I think Mike had practiced kissing other girls before me. He was two years older than I was. He always wanted me to let my hair out of its bun. When I did, he ran his fingers through my hair, telling me I was pretty, and I couldn't help but like that. I wrote this in my diary, next to "must work on extensions: devant, à la seconde."

As a teenager, I spent time at ballet schools, away from home. When we had a night off, I walked with Shandee and Maureen, two of my dormitory suite mates, to a local coffee shop and drank espresso. Under the guise of advice, Shandee said, "No one will want you in a company if you're a virgin."

I said that wasn't true.

"Sure it is," said Maureen.

"You only say it isn't true because you're still a virgin," added Shandee. She twirled a lock of her hair between her fingers, an affectation I had seen her use in the presence of men. Shandee liked the idea of men touching her. She told us as much. "It reminds me that I'm beautiful," she said.

Back home in LA, Maureen had a boyfriend who sent her letters full of the things he wanted to do to her, explicit and sexual. She read them aloud to make me uncomfortable.

Suzanne was our other dormitory suite mate. She smuggled a boy into her bedroom and bragged about how sore she was from this nocturnal visit. Part of me knew they were exaggerating for my benefit. But there was pressure: be womanly, be desirable, be the object of attention.

I didn't tell anyone that I was afraid. I panicked. Did anyone else really know I was a virgin? Would it keep me from being asked to join a company? So I worked harder in class, lost weight, followed the mantras I heard from teachers. Back in the dormitory, the girls harassed me. They nicknamed me Scarlet V. The Great Virgin Hope. They snickered about their sexual escapades in the backs of cars and dressing rooms. Shandee had a lover who was twenty-five. She was only sixteen. "He was shocked by the way I could bend," she bragged.

A girl got sent home from the ballet school. We were told she was abusing diet pills. We knew that couldn't be the true reason. Who would care if we abused diet pills, so long as we were skinny and doing well in class? The real reason she was sent home was because she was abusing speed. That was hushed, but we all knew. She was only seventeen.

Shandee asked, "How different is speed than diet pills?" I didn't use drugs, but I could understand why a dancer would. Speed increases alertness, energy. None of us were eating properly, and we were borderline anorexics or worse. Suzanne would splurge and purge: eat a dozen glazed donuts and then puke them up.

When I did lose my virginity, it was not to another dancer. As soon as it was lost, I wanted it back. But I knew I would never be pure, the way a dancer never feels truly beautiful or satisfied with herself. So I pushed: anorexia, extra coaching, makeup, practice, another class, Pilates, one more sit-up.

I didn't date very much; there was no time for it. The dates I did go on were awkward because I had nothing to say to boys who didn't understand ballet dancers, and these were the boys who asked me out. I didn't go out with male dancers: some were gay, and the others weren't appealing to me. It wouldn't be long before I attracted the attention of older men, those in the audience. Men confused me, younger and older. Their glances unnerved me. In many ways I was very naive. Perhaps I wanted to be naive.

Men. They were the choreographers, artistic directors, wealthy patrons. They commanded their little legions of women, and as dancers we willingly obeyed. We were vain creatures; we bought the hype. I was no exception. If a man wanted to sleep with me, I thought it was because I was a ballet dancer. I wanted them to want to sleep with me even though I didn't want to sleep with them. I was learning an ugly truth about ballet, that part of my success was being an object of desire.

Still, a part of me craved innocence. As a child, I had a wide smile, pigtails, and freckles. Now I missed the Sunday ice cream with my dad. I missed family life. Instead, I had rows of pointe shoes; cartons of baby powder; tubes of mascara; limp, damp tights with seams down the back. Strong lean legs. Long neck. A slim ponytail down the length of my back. Backstage, I received flowers from strange men.

In our dressing rooms, we peeled off parts of our costumes, skin still glistening from adrenaline and sweat. Partially exposed, we spilled in and out of the backstage rooms, talking or laughing, smoking cigarettes, maybe tending to blisters on our feet. There was wine, shots of vodka. The patrons were allowed backstage for parties put on by the company's management, ensuring that they would continue to write checks. They knew the patrons liked to see us this way, half naked, kissing cheeks in congratulation, preening, powdering, on display, a type of performance in itself.

In fourth position, place the heel of one foot against the middle of the other foot, keeping both turned out. Then slide the front foot forward, so there is space between the front and back foot. Fourth is crossed, but open. In this way, it is complicated.

In the ballet studio, everything about my physique was criticized. My body was always a work in progress. But when I took on extra work as a model at a local arts school, my perspective about my body shifted. Like other dancers I knew who modeled, I started because I needed the extra money. Behind a screen, I would take off my clothes and emerge completely nude to lie on a couch in the art studio. What is remarkable about this is that I was not embarrassed to do it. I was more comfortable unclothed in front of strangers than I was in a leotard and tights in the ballet studio. The artists studied me to recreate my form, while in the ballet studio just my form, just my body, would never do. In ballet, I was scrutinized without hope of ever reaching physical perfection. On the couch, there was no standard to live up to.

With my body spread across the couch, I was aware of the gazes of the art students only abstractly. Even though I was right there naked before them, it didn't feel like there was anyone in the room but me. I surprised myself with how relaxed I was. There wasn't any pressure to do anything other than to be drawn. I knew they would see me differently than the teachers, coaches, choreographers, and other dancers in the studio.

The art students never talked to me. I could hear the scratch of their pencils as they worked. I would find a glass of water and an envelope stuffed with cash waiting behind the screen with my clothes. Once, after I dressed and was walking across the studio to leave, I saw one of the drawings. The artist had left his large sketch pad on the easel. It shocked me: a swath of long hair, my stark, bony clavicle, and my breast, a tiny lump with an imperfect aureole, shaded darker but somehow more delicate in the individual strokes of the shading. In the center, a tense little nipple like a tightened fist.

I couldn't decide if it was beautiful or unbeautiful, but something in the depiction was both very close to me and so odd it couldn't have any connection to my body. I was affected by this picture, scared by it. What I remember in particular was practically running out to my car and driving away.

Yet I didn't stop posing. Seeing the picture made me bold, seeing myself differently through the drawing, a way I never saw myself as a dancer. Each week I came and undressed and displayed myself on the couch until the end of each class. I was almost happy to be there. Perhaps I thought that one day I would see one of these pictures, recognize it someplace I wouldn't expect. Maybe I would hear a person comment on the picture, something about beauty or grace. I had a tendency to romanticize, and I can only say that it was because my life as a ballet dancer was so unromantic that I desperately searched for it outside the studio.

But I didn't have any elaborate fantasies about how the artists saw me. Although the class was mostly young men, it didn't occur to me that they saw me as anything other than a subject to be drawn. After my last day as an artist's model, I walked behind the screen to dress. There, on top of my clothes, was a plain, white, three-by-five card. On the card, someone had written one sentence in almost perfectly symmetrical capital letters: *I ACHE FOR YOU.*

Every year, in every ballet company where I studied or performed, we put on the holiday classic *The Nutcracker.* The performances ensured revenues for the ballet company. As a dancer, it was a strange brew of holiday festivity and aching dread.

One year I was cast as Arabian, a short solo to slithering, reedy music, a moment of melancholy sensuality in this otherwise childlike ballet. In the particular choreography for my Arabian, which was a new rendition for that year, I was carried on stage by four male dancers, legs in a split. I danced between these men, lifted and turned and posed. What I didn't fully understand was that this particular choreographer had reinvented the part for me, for how he envisioned me.

I was surprised to be cast in Arabian because it was an

adagio, slow and sensual. I was never particularly good at adagio; I was more the spitfire. But I realize now that the reason I was chosen for this role was for my acting ability on stage more than my dancing. Typically, a soloist's role might really be a pas de deux, two dancers, one man and one woman together. In a pas de deux, there is an intimacy between the two dancers that the audience is allowed to watch. The ballerina captures the attention of her cavalier, and by extension the audience. My role in this particular adaptation of Arabian was to keep the attention of four men. But it could have been twenty men, it could have been every man who has ever been in a ballet audience and thought about what he might do if he was alone with the dancer. It was about sharing my body. At one point in Arabian, I snaked my leg around one of my partners in attitude while extending my arms out toward another. Here was my acting: I danced as if I knew what I was doing, which was seducing them.

I was never comfortable dancing Arabian, and I think my discomfort was something the choreographer wanted. There was always this paradox between innocence and sexuality. I was caught between them.

Often we would have parties backstage after *Nutcracker* performances. Our patrons threw them, the wings filled with cut veggies and little sweets, bottles of Chardonnay. After one evening of performing Arabian, at such a party, a man put his hand at the small of my back, a pressure in his fingers as he slid them around to caress my hip. I recognized him as a patron, but I didn't know him, and only knew he was much older than me. He complimented me on my performance onstage. What was implicit in this exchange was his pleasure. Maybe what he saw on stage made him think of his own bedroom, lights low, arranging a dancer on his bed, her warm, slight body against the coolness of sheets, his hands posing her to his liking. A part of me knew this. I saw this attention as a curse. But as a ballet dancer, if I wasn't desirable, I was a failure. So if I was disgusted, I was also pleased. What I didn't understand at the time was how anonymous it all was. I could have been any dancer on stage. For him, I was just any dancer. And, I was okay with being just any dancer, as long as I was one.

Balanchine's philosophy: God creates. Woman inspires. Man assembles. He said, "The ballet is a purely female thing; it is a woman, a garden of beautiful flowers, and man is the gardener."

Oh, really, Mr. B.? God had nothing to do with it.

FIFTH

A Russian proverb: acknowledgment is half of correction. Like many dancers, I found refuge in technique. I had moments that were just dancing. Stolen moments. Usually jumping, spinning, leaping. If you said the steps aloud just right, you felt the lilt and bounce. Glissade, brisé: legs like skipping in delicate figure eights. Assemblé: breathe, release, travel across the floor. Quick and light. Like air. Like a breeze—brisé. I gave up my cares when I performed the petit allegro, even in class. In those steps, I was more than myself, my drive, my passions, my mirror. I forgot to think. I just danced in fast, skittering movements across the floor. I felt perfect for one shining minute of music.

One day I stood in front of the mirror, working out a combination. I gave myself to the steps, concentrating. It was a day when I didn't pay attention to the other dancers around me. It was a day to study my own self, my own body. That was a good day.

Another day the teacher from Hamburg Ballet said, "Look at her clean beats" as I jumped through the steps of a petit allegro. My feet were speedy; they cut the air in brisk strokes. I smiled. It was a day when the mirror didn't feel like an attack.

The choreographer Twyla Tharp said, "Dancing is like bank robbery, it takes split-second timing."

I still struggled through the adagio, the slow controlled extensions, the movements that require a different kind of precision, a meticulous, cultivated sense of line. Strong and delicate, the adagio requires embracing opposites: static fluidity. It requires a maturity and patience that I didn't own, that I could only achieve through affectation. But imitation was part of my craft as a ballet dancer. Allegra Kent, one of Balanchine's muses, said, "All we actually have is our body and its muscles that allow us to be under our own power."

Balanchine has been dead for most of my life. But his influence over every American dancer who came after he started his School of American Ballet has been absolute. We all danced for him, in his image of woman: lean, whittled, yet erotic. He was the one who first demanded the slim physique, so slight in frame. But despite its delicacy, it also had to be powerful enough to move with the quickness of racehorses. When he started the School of American Ballet, he created a stable of dancers, like a breeder of champion thoroughbreds.

I continued to chase Balanchine's ideal. So I found a coach—Jilise Austin—a redheaded beauty who used to be with his New York City Ballet. Jilise pushed me beyond what I thought were my limits, which was what I wanted her to do. I needed to be pushed. I ached to be pushed.

Ballet was about pursuit.

Under her tutelage, I felt my body lengthening, felt the line of my body as an energy that ran from my fingers through my arms into my spine. From my toe through my calf and my thigh. Jilise also knew how to accentuate a dancer's strongest points. We worked through combinations of petit allegro: faster, faster, sharper, faster, like little sparks of light at the end of my legs. I was stronger on my left side than right, so we worked on partnering, which required a strong left foot.

I continued to seek out mentors. In pas de deux I was coached by a Polish dancer who had trained in Russia. He spoke six and a half languages, English the half language. We were working on a complex lift, and he tried to say don't be scared. But it came out, "Oh, don't be scary!"

Never satisfied with my progress, I spent more time being coached by Jilise. With her, I felt the direct connection back to Balanchine, because she taught from the experience of being trained directly by him. With this knowledge, she worked out the kinks in my technique, mostly my arms, the way I carried myself, the way my shoulders and upper body appeared. "Shoulders down, resist the tension in the back muscles," she said. Energy from the ring finger through the elbow to the shoulder. Elbow relaxed. Lift up from the sternum. In such commands, grace was acquired.

"You should wear white," Jilise said. "You look perfect in white. Maybe someday you will be Giselle or Odette." But that day never came. I was neither. In the end, I did not even merit a footnote in the world of ballet. But I learned from Jilise that a dancer sacrifices everything for the chance. She believed Mr. B., as she knew Balanchine, when he said, "I don't want people who want to dance, I want people who have to dance."

Ballet sets a nearly impossible standard. It is erotic. Beguiling. Sexy. Demure. Slender. Extended. Driven. A composed surface, insecurity underneath. As a dancer, I loved and hated myself.

In fifth position, the legs fit and lock together. Turning out from the hips is key. Toe to heel, heel to toe. You can turn, you can leap, but you are, from that point forward, made from dance.

Never Famous

ENTER THE BLANK ROOM: walls flanked by two levels of barres except the one wall of mirror. Sometimes you must study what's reflected; other times you must ignore it. Eyes deceive, especially your own eyes upon your own form. Breathe. Demi plié. It's a way to begin. Work the foot: crease to demi-pointe, feel the instep. Stretch to full pointe. Don't crunch the toes. Crease again. You are waking the muscles of the foot. Warm up the body from the feet up to the head. Slow. Methodical. Maybe light filters in through a window. Maybe you're in a box. It could be raining or snowing outside. Sun shining bright. In here, weather doesn't exist. This is the atmosphere of music. 4/4. 6/8. Allegro. Adagio. Waltz. You're here for hours. Six, eight, ten, more. You repeat combinations over and over. Lots of posing in lines. Then move. Go! Your body tires. Dance harder. Sweat beads, drips, dries. You sweat again. Layer in sweatshirts and leg warmers between one studio and another, strip them off as you move again, glissade arabesque. You snack on fruit, lunch on tuna, drink Diet Coke for the rush of caffeine. Whatever keeps you trim but keeps you going. Tea, coffee, Advil. Your eyes tell all. Sorrow, elation, frustration, tiredness. Your hair is pulled from your face, pulled and pinned in a knot. This emphasizes the eyes even more. Wear mascara if you think it helps. Sew ribbons and elastics on shoes during breaks. Read paperbacks you swap with others. Read paperbacks your mother sends in care packages. Keep medical tape and Band-Aids in your bag. Sprinkle baby powder, but not perfume. Pack extra everything: shoes, tights, leotard, bobby pins, T-shirts. Bring a chiffon skirt if you need to feel pretty. Sometimes you just need to feel pretty. Take barre next to dancers better than you. Practice. Practice more. Pray. There are a few things I know for sure. Ballet is work. The work is beautiful and often thankless. Some performances you get flowers. Other times you don't. Mostly you rehearse. There are no flowers for rehearsal. Most dancers are never famous. Don't worry about that. Dance like you are the most beautiful creature that ever existed, even when—no—especially when your practice tutu is dirty and your pointe shoes are dead and you feel all but spent.

Raked Stages: A Twelve-Step Program

1. HOW I REIMAGINE RUSSIA: a girl with two low pigtails, dressed in a pink leotard and white socks folded at the ankles; her feet tucked into white slippers, shuffling against the floor as she sprinkled it with a watering can. Her face was the delicate pink of the insides of shells, soft, light, almost translucent. Her hair was dark, darker than my own, polished ebony. She was preparing the room for class, wetting the floor for traction.

A dirty light filtered through a filthy window. No one cared. The girls filed in and helped each other stretch. The girls had perfect turnout. Their faces were serious; not smiling, just concentrated. Their faces were scrubbed to a rosy shine.

What I also remember is color. Russia was full of peacock blues and bruised purples and tarnished silver. The colors of an eerie feeling, like the sun had turned to ash but never set.

2. You and I, Aleda, sat on my patio in Morgantown, West Virginia. "You should write about that," you said. "The raked stages. And about drinking Tab and smoking."

Actually, what you said was "You should write a poem about that." And so I got it half right, which is about as right as I can get it. The difference between a poet and a ballet dancer comes down to these essentials: a poet distills and refines the magic of language. She has faith. A ballet dancer distills and refines her body, which resists magic. She believes only what she can see and feel.

You reminded me of a small band of gypsies I once encountered. Your hair pulled back beneath a bright pink Hermès scarf; you carried an expensive-looking, red, pebbled leather bag with smart hardware. You wore fabulous black kitten-heeled shoes. Perhaps you were a gypsy in haute couture. Because, like the gypsies, you had the ability to watch, to see, to capture something true and fundamental about a person, even one you didn't know well. Perhaps you saw best without trusting your eyes.

3. My first Russian word was *nyet*. It was unmistakable. My main teacher was Lyudmila, who spoke very little English. When she corrected me, which was often, she cawed, "*Nyet*! *Nyet*!" and followed it with what she must have thought was intelligible English. Then she slipped into French. The French, I think, was mostly swearing. Thankfully, my French was not so good.

I would not be a ballet dancer if I were Russian. Or, if somehow I had slipped in, I would probably have been shipped off to do folk dancing in one of the provinces, like Armenia. I would say Siberia, but that's too easy. A gulag of failed dancers in Siberia was not as interesting as being shipped off to Armenia, which somehow, unexplainably, felt more like reality. A so-called Zen place for my failure as a ballerina.

Lyudmila squawked about my turnout—it really wasn't much different from what I'd heard before. Ballet has these constants. My American teachers squawked about my turnout—and in English, and in terms I definitely understood. "You have to turn out from the hips, the hips! You know what those are, don't you?" I sometimes wondered. I would stretch my hip sockets, working to loosen the joint, but, still, I never had perfect turnout. Over and over I was told, "Turn out more." All of these teachers who asked me for better turnout were tiny women, delicate-faced and, of course, perfectly turned out themselves. Perfect ballet bodies. Brutal in their corrections.

Lyudmila's nostrils flared when she was excited, and somehow even this gesture had a kind of grace to it. Her corrections to me were agitated, as if she were incensed not just with me but the whole American system of teaching dancers. I promised Lyudmila that I'd work harder. All dancers promise this to their teachers. It's our pact.

4. My room was bugged. I lived in a boardinghouse that was within walking distance of the school. Our landlady, Vera, ran the house, cooked the meals and, in the beginning, walked us to classes. Early on, I had a small withdrawal problem—there was no Tab in Russia, my favorite beverage. I drank no less than three a day back home, hooked on the caffeine. So I had to learn to drink coffee—cold coffee. It was 1989, and there had been words—*perestroika, glasnost*—but there was a Soviet conscience at work.

I heard the microphone's low crackle at night before I fell asleep. I imagined KGB officers listening to me in my room. They must have thought I was absolutely boring. They weren't getting some beautiful spy girl, James Bond–style, sent with a wink to pose as a ballet student. What the KGB heard was almost sad: in my free time, I mostly talked to myself about corrections, wrote letters home, and stretched or practiced relevés. I played Prince on my bright yellow Sony Sports Walkman that a man on the street had tried to buy from me. He had also asked to buy my jeans and any tampons I might have. This man knew I was American. I never told him; it was obvious. He said he could get me vodka and Bulgarian cigarettes. Also, KGB paraphernalia. The black market had strange demands, strange rewards, but I didn't make the deal.

5. The truth about Russia: there's no way through. For me, Russia will always be the beautiful failure of my dancing. But even failures can have a remarkable kind of beauty, especially in hindsight.

6. In class, Lyudmila was surprised to find I could jump. I had ballon. Her eyes widened and she pinched my cheek. She had a nickname for me that I couldn't translate, because my Russian vocabulary was limited to "nyet."

I made a Russian friend. Anya. She was in my class, a striking beauty. Anya had the whitest skin I'd ever seen, so white it actually looked fragile pale blue. Her eyes were large and nearly black, and she reminded me of a Madame Alexander doll, very sweet and slightly creepy and somehow also pretty, pretty but almost wicked. Pretty like sin. But I didn't tell her this because she might have been offended, or she might not have known what a Madame Alexander doll was, because how could she? I didn't think there were any in Russia, which was ironic, because Madame Alexander was, of all things, a Russian immigrant. Anya was all long limbs, which was the part of her not like a Madame Alexander doll. Those dolls were chubby-looking, the way, I suppose, their maker pictured spoiled little girls. Anya was not chubby. Her face was long and thin, like the rest of her. She had perfect turnout and high, graceful, effortless extensions, and excelled in adagio work. I often thought the Russian word for adagio ought to be "Anya."

Anya's English was much better than the teachers'. "Your nickname means 'Little Potato,' " she explained to me.

I was crushed. Folk dancing in Armenia: I imagined mountain roads and puffy skirts and lots of mazurkas. Little Potato, that was me. I saw myself as a Mr. Potato Head toy, one with big bright lips, the tulle of a violet sugar plum tutu sprouting where my waist had turned into a great brown lump.

7. Anya and I began to walk home together after classes. She spoke her wonderful broken English, which left me a little confused, but it was clear enough that I could have conversation, which I desperately needed. There were seven girls from the United States here in Moscow as part of an exchange program, but none of us were friends. Back home we would all be competing for spots at summer intensives and in ballet companies. We couldn't afford to be friends, not even abroad, and especially not Katie and me. Katie was another girl in the exchange program. We had spent the summer before in the same division at a reputable and highly competitive ballet school, both of us hacking it out against each other to be considered something better than mediocre. Katie had naturally curly hair, and it sprung at the temples in class when she started to sweat. She had nice turnout but couldn't jump. I knew her faults, she knew mine.

Anya lived on the same street as the boardinghouse where I stayed. It was a small one-bedroom apartment she shared with her aunt who was unmarried and worked, as far as I could discern from Anya's descriptions, as a low-level diplomat's administrative assistant. I often wondered if Anya's aunt worked for the poor son of a bitch who was tasked with monitoring the bug in my room. "She's talking to herself again," I imagined him sighing, only to have an interpreter tell him that I was reciting ballet corrections.

On our walks Anya liked to smoke—the Bolshoi girls liked Bulgarian cigarettes, and Anya had told me I should have traded for them. "Hard to get," she said. "Very expensive." She liked to listen to my bright yellow Sony Sports Walkman, especially *Purple Rain*, which I'll admit was my favorite, too. We sang along to "Baby I'm a Star."

At the bridge we stopped. One day, without warning, there was a collection of people, mostly women, one very old and missing a front tooth on the bottom row. A pretty young girl, with toffee-colored hair to her waist and a long skirt, collected rubles from those who crossed the bridge. Anya pulled out her toll, and I reached for my wallet and the old woman with the missing tooth began to screech, a sound that I think was meant to be words but sounded like an angry peacock.

I thought, *of course that crazy woman was missing a tooth.* What a stupid clichéd thing. Staged, I was sure. I believed it was all a rouse for the silly American girl trying to learn ballet.

The toffee-haired girl spoke in rapid sentences to Anya, who responded but looked bewildered, her skin looking even a little bluer than before. She turned to me and said, "They don't take your money."

"What?" I asked.

"They don't take your money," Anya repeated.

"Why?" I demanded.

"Gypsies say magic not work on you." Anya looked concerned, but her voice was as low and flat as I had become accustomed to.

I studied these gypsies, as most of them had pulled back away from us, as if I were sick and contagious—how I think people in medieval times might have acted toward those with the plague. The old woman cackled, and I got the impression that there was something wrong with me. Very wrong. But I didn't ask. I thought that whatever it was it had to be why I was a mediocre dancer who'd been nicknamed Little Potato. Russia conspired against me.

We moved along.

"I never know no one who doesn't pay the gypsies," Anya said, after we were well past the bridge and nearing my building.

I scraped my feet on the pavement, just to hear the sound. Then I answered, "We don't have gypsies in America."

Every time I crossed the bridge, the gypsies eyed me, suspicious, perhaps wary. I wanted to think of myself as some sort of gypsy-master, a girl who would not be thwarted by them. But when I'm honest, I can admit that I was upset at these gypsies. What had I ever done to them? The gypsies made me feel abnormal. And I already felt clumsy and out of place. I thought, *Stupid gypsies, with your stupid magic.* I thought, *I don't believe in your magic anyway.*

The gypsies, I think, knew better.

Sometimes I wonder what to do with what I remember. I am not at all sure by which threads our memories are strung together. But this memory of the gypsies makes me think of an expensive-looking, red, pebbled leather bag with smart hardware, which I want to believe was really full of secrets.

And it makes me wonder, did you believe in gypsies, Aleda? I think you did. I want to believe in gypsies, and magic, but then again I don't want to believe, because I don't want to be left out.

What's easier for me to believe in are the things that I can feel. And so, I believe in pain. When I was a dancer, my body ached all the time—pulled muscles or knotted ones, swelling joints, or just a dull ache all over. It's the ache I remember—a very particular ache, but one that was comforting. I took my pain and believed it made me beautiful. It wasn't magic, it was real. That's what I told myself.

Of course, the gypsies knew better. Maybe you knew better, too.

8. I have a very odd history with the beet. I never ate beets, but I loved beet eggs—bright purple and pickled.

Vera made our meals and one night she made borscht. I'd never had borscht; I didn't even know what it was, but when I tasted it, oh, how delicious. Vera said, "It's from Ukraine." This, I understood, meant Vera was from the Ukraine. I wondered how she was living in Moscow, found it ironic that she wasn't in Kiev, hosting girls with the Kirov instead of being here with girls at the Bolshoi. It seemed all turned around. I didn't even think of it in terms of the United States—where I had moved from North Dakota to West Virginia to Florida, and then studied in Michigan and Milwaukee and New York and all sorts of places in between. The odd thing about being in a foreign country was the static feeling. I couldn't conceive of the people I met in Russia ever moving someplace else in the country. Like they were somehow fixed, like the little mechanical figures dressed in ethnic costumes in the "It's a Small World" ride at Disney World.

We ate hot borscht. Vera told me, "Can also serve cold," on my second helping, an occurrence that had not happened before with her American wards. We were all dancers, one portion eaters, if that.

I asked, "This is made with beets?"

Vera replied, "Also has cabbage." It was like stew, served with bread topped with fresh garlic. I had another helping.

"You're going to get fat," said Katie, who'd barely touched hers. We'd learned to watch each other in the cafeteria in the Rose Building when we were at School of American Ballet, taking inventory of what every other student ate, adding calories and pounds in our heads. We were better spies than the agents who bugged our building. We had the goods on each other.

I wanted to say, "You're already fat." I didn't say it. I remembered something else. "Well," I said to Katie, "I was never the one who our teacher said couldn't jump." I ate the rest of my borscht. Vera beamed, the only time I saw her smile. It was actually an eerie smile, more smug than happy. I reeked of garlic.

Not long after this, Lyudmila sent a note home with me for Vera. I asked Anya to translate: *stop feeding the American girls borscht.* I wondered how she knew, but somehow I have an idea of who ratted me out. Vera was not amused either. All she made after that, it seemed, were omelets and, occasionally, little mincemeat pastries, which I didn't like at all.

9. Sometimes we American girls were taken on tours. This was explained to us as part of our exchange, a way to understand the local culture. Once we went to see Lenin's body. I had imagined this would be a disturbing experience, but when I looked at him, embalmed, preserved, I couldn't

feel anything. Lenin didn't even look real. I was shocked
that I didn't feel horrified or reverent or anything. I thought
about the gypsies and wondered if this was why their magic
never worked on me—maybe magic, in general, was beyond
my grasp.

It made me think about what we did on stage, how
dancers represented ideas—or maybe more accurately,
ideals—sylphs, nymphs, fairies. Imagined women. Maybe
my problems in the studio stemmed from not being attuned
to magic, and thus my body rejected the movements of
ethereal magical creatures. Maybe if ballet dancers were
gremlins, elves, gnomes, and imps, I would have been better
suited. Even gypsies. I wanted to blame my bridge's gypsies
and Lenin's preserved body, but the problem was me. The
problem has always been me. I've never just believed. I
lacked faith. Many times I had heard in ballet class, "Just
do, don't *think* so much." Thinking was made out to be the
death of dancers. I was slowly killing myself.

Of course, more famous people had talked about this
dancing/thinking problem. I remember a moment of clarity
while reading *Dancing on My Grave*. Apparently, Gelsey
Kirkland was also an overthinker. At least, that is what she
claimed. Part of me discounted her because she was so close
to ballet's ideal, so nearly perfect, and I was nowhere near
that perfection. I was barely good enough, with a body that
wasn't bad enough to hold me back, and not correct enough
to do what it really needed to do. And maybe because I was
only barely good enough, I wanted to think of her confession as overly dramatic. This was the way of my envy. But
what ballet dancer didn't envy Gelsey Kirkland?

Which brings me to my tour of the Bolshoi Theatre. It
was also part of our cultural enlightenment, but one that
was much more exciting than seeing the embalmed body of

Lenin. The theater was smaller than I expected, but beautiful. I remember the balconies catching my eye, but what captured my attention most were the raked, or sloped, stages. Gelsey Kirkland had talked about them like they were the dancer's equivalent of a terrible road hazard—something that sends you toppling off the highway and flip-flopping over yourself. I decided I didn't trust her and I was going to find out for myself. They let us walk across the stage, where I slipped off my shoes—I intentionally had worn clogs so it would be easy to slip them off. I took fourth position, prepared for a simple pirouette. I rose up onto my leg, the other neatly pulled up into retiré, and spotted the turn and . . . whack!

My butt smacked against the stage with force. Just like Gelsey Kirkland had said, I couldn't find my equilibrium, and then couldn't balance. I thought I was going to spin headlong into the front row of empty seats. Sure, I'd felt the slope, but I hadn't trusted that it would throw me off. I was cocky—something I usually wasn't in the ballet studio. Maybe I just wanted to prove Gelsey Kirkland wrong, or maybe I wanted to feel like I could do something, any one little thing, that she couldn't.

My understanding was that the stages were raked so that the audience could better view all the action, both upstage and downstage. I could only imagine what a series of turns and leaps might feel like coming down stage, gathering force and momentum from the decline. But for the audience, the raked stage helped create the magic, helped create the world of the stage. Once again, I didn't tap into the magic. I was a nonbeliever.

Raked stages: you'd have to get used to them and adjust, but there's something even more basic than that. It does have to do with the magic on stage. I've been looking for the magic my whole life, and yet when I'm presented with evidence of it, I turn away, or fall on my ass.

10. And then, of course, there was a boy; there's always a boy. His name was Mikhail—Misha—but I had to call him Little Misha because in my mind, Mikhail—Misha—meant Mikhail Baryshnikov. I never knew *that* Misha personally, although everyone in the dance world referred to him by this nickname, like we were all friends. It was ironic, too, that I called him "little," because he was taller than the famous Misha, who was notoriously compact.

Little Misha started walking home with Anya and me, and it was Anya who first said, "I think he likes you." I invited Anya and Little Misha to come over to the room where I stayed, and we played Prince on my Walkman and passed around the earphones. And then one day Anya stopped coming. She said, "I have to get home to my aunt," when we reached the boardinghouse, and then only Little Misha came in with me, Vera suspiciously eyeing him, barking hello in Russian.

Maybe it was because I was in a foreign country and maybe he was just that handsome, but I was surprised that Little Misha liked me and that I liked him. I never dated dancers—either I wasn't interested or they weren't interested or they were gay, openly or closeted—and I hardly dated back then at all. But I suppose that everything was different in a foreign country. Little Misha had green eyes and dark hair and a brooding way about him that struck me as sexy, even though I really wasn't old enough to understand what sexy really was.

At first, we sat in my room and shared the earphones and

listened to music. I also had brought the Cure, the Smiths, Echo and Bunnymen, and Duran Duran, which was out of date but still a favorite.

Then we listened to Prince.

Even with a Russian teenager who was just slightly older than me, and who spoke minimal English, he got the point of the songs. Especially, Prince. Particularly when we'd been listening to fairly popular songs like "When Doves Cry" and then we listened to songs like "Darling Nikki." Like sex oozing through the Walkman into the earphones, it translated, and suddenly, I was kissing Little Misha.

This should have been thrilling—after all, the only other boy I'd kissed was Mike, the trumpet player at Interlochen Arts Academy. Kissing boys was supposed to be something exciting for sixteen-year-old girls, even dancers. Maybe kissing a trumpet player spoils a girl. The problem was that Little Misha was a terrible kisser. He was a well-trained and talented dancer with a great physique—as dancers we spent our days in the tightest of clothes, where, perhaps, the nickname Little Misha proved to be the most inaccurate. He could leap higher than any other boy in his division, but his idea of kissing was basically to stick his tongue in my mouth and wait for me to kiss back. His lips were limp. But worse, they were wet, slobbery wet, boy wet in the worst way. I got a ring of saliva around my mouth that made me shudder. I was disgusted. In late 1980s teen vernacular: I was, like, totally grossed out.

Little Misha misinterpreted my shudder as one of pleasure and his fingers tried to work the zipper of my jeans—the jeans that the guy I met who worked the black market tried to get me to sell him, for both vodka and Bulgarian cigarettes, which might, in fact, have helped in this situation.

I pulled away and immediately pressed the stop button on

the Walkman. Little Misha looked at me, like I'd kneed him in the groin during a botched supported pirouette. He yelled something at me in Russian and stomped around. Famous Russian temper, I thought. I wanted to be upset, too, but I was relieved. I got up and went to the bathroom I shared with the other girls in the boardinghouse and washed my face, several times, lathering the soap, letting the water get as hot as I could stand it. I scrubbed and scrubbed. By the time I returned to my room, Little Misha was gone.

I was sure there was going to be fallout in the studios the next day, but Anya insisted there was nothing damaging about me in the school's gossip. She said all that Little Misha had said was, "American girls are fun, but they will never be good dancers." I didn't even get mad about it. Although I have always wondered if Anya was telling me the whole truth. Despite this, she and I went back to walking home together and listening to music until it was evening and she was expected at her aunt's apartment.

11. During the last week I was in Russia, Lyudmila liked me better. She even said Little Potato in a softer tone, which betrayed her fondness, as if she believed that if she just had more time with me, she could turn me into a dancer that maybe, just maybe, wouldn't be sent off to Armenia for folk dancing. She would gently prod me, tapping my Achilles heel lightly with her index finger, and I would try my best, inching my extension a tiny bit higher, wishing of course, that I might please her. I promised to keep working on my turnout and my extensions when I returned home.

"You promise," she said and sounded a little sad, even though she still flared her nostrils.

During that last week, Anya and I didn't listen to music. We sat in my room, staring at my bed, sitting slumped against the wall with our legs flopped in front of us. She would sniffle but never cry, and I only cried after she left. I had no Anya in the United States, and if I did, we wouldn't be friends. We could only be friends here because we really weren't competing. We would have never competed anyway; she was a much better dancer than I would ever be, and a year younger, too. Before I left, I gave her a pair of my jeans and my tampons and my Walkman and made her promise that she would never sell them on the black market, no matter what the cost of Bulgarian cigarettes. I said I'd come back and she said she'd come to the United States, and both of us knew neither would ever happen.

The colors of Russia are like a bruise, and the bruise is on my heart and never goes away. In my ear I still hear the soft incantation: *nyet, nyet*. I wish I'd tried to pirouette again on the raked stages of the Bolshoi. I can see the red velvet seats in the audience, the gold tassels on the stage's heavy curtains.

The night before I left Russia, Vera made me borscht. "No complaining now," she said on my second helping. We left early the next morning. I thought Vera would be up to make us breakfast, but we ate on the plane. It makes me sad when I remember that I never got to say goodbye to her. To tell the truth, I've never been any good at goodbyes. But I'm good at remembering.

12. The colors of Russia: ashy patinas over deep purples, velvet blues. The colors of you: bright pinks and bold reds. The color of me: white; the color of the sylphs and swans and willis of classical ballet, the hot light of the stage, the absence of all color.

This story should have ended with goodbye.

But when I'm remembering I can't help but to imagine Russia, and I can see myself there now. In my imagined Russia, I eat Vera's delicious borscht and, of course, never gain any weight. Anya meets me at the boardinghouse. She is still painfully beautiful. We trace our old route; Anya leads, taking me to the bridge we always crossed. The old woman with the missing tooth smiles and cackles, but I'm not mad at her anymore. The rest of her clan looks at us, not accusing, not scared, but curious. I put my hand in the old woman's, give her my money, and command, "Gypsy, work your magic."

Coda: Partnering

YOUR PARTNER KNOWS YOUR BODY better than any of your lovers. He knows your means and hows, your hollows and crevices, how your weight is distributed through bust and hips and thighs. He doesn't make fun of your large potato head or your stick-y-out ears. When you dance together, his sweat and your sweat mix, no way to tell who has perspired what.

You both sweat all through rehearsals.

He admires your strong, flexible feet and your strong, flexible back. You learn to trust that extra rotation, the flying leap that's caught in air. Most of the time, you trust your partner more than you trust yourself.

The art of partnering is a lot like love, the coming together of two beings, two bodies. These bodies, yours and your partner's, are honed with technique and purpose and work. You condition it with daily class, daily rehearsals, daily regimens, your diet, your bottle upon bottle of water. Your partner takes the same classes, attends the same rehearsals, carries out his own rituals and regimens. You respect that about one another. You respect what is physical, and you use it to reveal what is sublime. He will hold your waist, circle your wrists with his hands. He will cradle your body, grip your thighs. It isn't sexual, but it can be sexy. The thrill is creating something beautiful, as if beauty was something you do, not something you are.

In the low light of an expiring day, you will remember this, think of your partner more fondly than your past lovers. You will wonder where he went after you left the stage, what new and lovely creatures he supported and lifted and spun. You will not be jealous; rather, you will wish you could have seen these performances, your body humming with past knowledge. The sun will sink. It will rise again in pink streaks across a slate of indifferent sky.

Out of the Blue

SHORTHAND, WE JUST CALLED IT "Bluebird," but technically the role was Princess Florina. Hers is the tale of a maiden who wanted to learn to fly, and about the prince, disguised as the bluebird who taught her. For the celebration of Aurora's wedding in the third act of *Sleeping Beauty,* the Bluebird story, compressed, became entertainment for both onstage wedding guests and audience members. Bluebird was a common choice to teach young dancers advanced enough learn some repertoire. Reminded of many famous dancers who made their soloist debuts as Princess Florina, when given the role in a showcase, I thought of it as a sign of things to come.

My costume, royal blue with feathers on the platter tutu as well as a feathered headpiece, did make me feel a bit like a delicate bird. Wanting to stroke the feathers with my fingers, I learned restraint by not mussing my costume, resisting the urge to pet and caress. In a platter tutu, I felt like a real dancer. Platter tutus signified a rite of passage, at least for me, and still, when I see young dancers in platter tutus, I feel a little nostalgia for my royal blue beginnings. As a very young girl I'd had a Barbie doll that came in a platter tutu and with crown permanently attached to her head, which I adored until I realized Barbie dolls are made so they have no turnout, and ballet is based on turning out by rotating from the hips. Barbie's leg only swung back to front. Barbie could never have been a dancer, not for real, but in my tutu, I thought perhaps I was a dancer.

The bodice of my costume had a long series of hooks and, when one of the backstage dressers helped clasp them, I imagined what it must have been like to wear a corset. Made with stiff boning, the bodice restricted my middle, binding me in and making it hard to breathe. And yet I liked that about it, believing because it was unforgiving it made my dancing somehow better, pain and beauty intertwined into a mythically enhanced concoction.

Costuming aside, Florina challenged me in other ways. Although I excelled at petit allegro, which was needed for the part, Princess Florina was not the kind of role I'd expected to get. The role called for lightheartedness, a term I would not use to describe either my technique or my personality; the motivation behind the steps was that of flight, learning to fly. Florina, the little flora, a tiny and fresh and lovely princess. In my naive early days of performing, I felt challenged to be the role I was given—whether something in *The Nutcracker*, or a part of the *Waltz of the Hours*, I didn't just want to dance my roles. I wanted to become them. Because I didn't see myself as a Princess Florina, I found it tough to be her. My other early roles were icy, winter-infused parts,

Snowflake and Winter Fairy, and I cultivated the persona. Florina challenged my very sense of self, and I struggled.

Choreography can be a map, and the steps in the Florina variation helped me—as if tripping forward in bourrées and flittering échappés, light and nearly flickering piqué fouetté, then bourrées again. What message could I find hidden in the architecture of the steps themselves? What I physically did became who I would be. For me, a princess, regal, mimicking a bird, airy with flight. The steps aimed to reconcile the two competing characters in my body, if it was up to the task.

The full tale of Florina, not entirely depicted as part of the celebration of Aurora's wedding, goes something like this. A king has a daughter in a first marriage—Florina—who, during her father's second marriage gets locked in a tower by her stepmother, who had an ugly daughter she wanted married off. Fearing Florina would capture the hearts of suitors, off went Florina—standard fare for this kind of story. Pretty girls are always getting locked up for the mere offense of being attractive. A prince, enamored with Florina and disguised as Bluebird, comes to her window in her tower prison. Of course, Florina can't tell he's a prince.

Can we ever tell who the princes are?

The Bluebird visits Florina in captivity, bringing her presents, and she, growing fond of him, caresses his wings and feathers. The queen, Florina's stepmother, finds out about the Bluebird visits, and closes the window to Florina's chamber, keeping Bluebird out, but Florina sings out for him.

In the *Sleeping Beauty* version, the choreography imitates Florina's call to Bluebird. The ending pose of the variation—on one knee, hand behind the ear—the dancer indicates call and response. The trick was making it look effortless, piqué arabesque, and then the gentle kneel, soft swish of arms to the listening pose. Delicate, I struggled with the pose in rehearsal. My arms beckoned, "Get here, bird," instead of the gentle "Where are you? Please come to me."

My coach, a former soloist with the Hamburg Ballet, kept correcting me with an incantation of "Soft, soft, soft. Don't plunk down."

In order to free Florina, Bluebird teaches her to fly, so they can travel aloft, destined for those places where fairy-tale characters live happily ever after. To say I thought about this learning the pas de deux, the variation, or the coda for Florina would be a lie. But the effect was there, embedded in the steps. What I didn't know or understand was some-times gifted to me in the dance itself.

The coda, the flight: my partner danced, arms replicat-ing flight, and I entered in the upstage corner as he rotated through multiple pirouettes. Light piqué turns from the corner, single, double, single, double. Chaînés in canon, first him, then me, graceful instruction. It wasn't unlike actual birds, which alight on a perch, hop, or take flight, only to perch again. Each step interpreted the weightless, skittering movements of actual birds, but with the elegance intrinsic to ballet. Harder to accomplish, too, since they also were bound and confined by the demands of ballet technique. Still only a teenager and apprentice dancer, I performed pieces from the ballets felt complicated in a way I couldn't quite explain at the time. The birds did what they did natu-rally; for me, Florina's movements contained a joie de vivre that I found alien. Who trapped in a tower would be so happy? Could the idea of flight insight such sense of joy? Still, I took on Florina for what it was, and I loved the role simply because it was difficult.

Later, I would understand the obstacles of Princess Florina in a different way. Lightheartedness seemed so elusive and, even now, I'm not sure exactly how to capture her easy effervescence To be lighthearted means to cast away cares and worries, and I have never, and still do not, shed these easily.

In my royal and feathered tutu, the light around me took on a bluish tinge, and I became something other than myself. It's the release that created the performance high. Unlike any other feeling I have known, it was as if for that moment I slipped underneath someone else's skin. There, I could be fresh and lovely, the likeness of Florina.

Words will never capture performance adequately. Of the sensations I most remember, there was the heat of the stage's lights on my skin, compared to the cool dampness of the backstage. Also, the look and feel of my costumes, which have always stayed more vivid in my memories and imagination than any pirouette or jump or extension of my leg. What I did was gone the moment I did it. Performing disappears as it happens, a vapor, a curl of smoke, a waking dream. And even if I emerged out of this blue-hazed memory more like Florina trapped in her tower than Florina in flight, I had ahead of me the task of trying to commit memory to words, a fairy tale itself, daring to dream again of my own past.

Part II

A Woman Tethered to the Earth

Hair: A Short History

WHEN FORCED TO QUIT DANCING, you did the only thing you could: you cut your hair. A bold act, the length of long, silky brown became a short, stark bob. A flapper for the 1990s. An act of rebellion against the feature that so tied you to the look of a ballet dancer. The shortened hair made you look even younger than you were, but you didn't care. You didn't look like someone who belonged in a dance studio, but you needed to move on. Your body would take a longer time to change, but let's not get ahead.

The ballerina Darci Kistler had long blond hair, commented on so often by others that it became iconographic. One of your early idols, Darci Kistler became your standard of beauty. When, at a summer intensive, a teacher remarked that your hair reminded her of a brunette version of Kistler, you nearly died of delight. So when the locks fell, perhaps you should have cried. But you didn't. That time was over, passed. Cutting allowed you to move along.

The short hair, much to your hairdresser's surprise, pleased you. You didn't resemble your old self very much with the cropped look, but a different young woman who could be anything: a teacher, a businesswoman, a personal trainer, a scientist, a therapist, a programmer, a fashion designer. You wanted to be a writer. Newly minted with the short locks and "I can do anything" attitude, you didn't write about dance. At first, you wrote about fishing: with your family in surf off the Atlantic, with two old guys at the reservoir. You owned a pink rod the color of a Daisy razor, the kind you shaved your legs with. You didn't know much at all about fishing, but you went out with the two old guys and a Yorkie named Odie. Mostly, they told you stories. One owned the bait shop on the reservoir, which kept losing letters, so it was the "IT SHOP."

Still, inside you, there was the training of a ballet dancer.

The disease had its own mind and pace, and for a while, that pace was aggressive. Later there would be more effective ways to control it. But for years you felt its effects every day, wondered if there would be a day that your body—filled out more since quitting dance but still slender—wouldn't feel sluggish, filled with fluid. You never said hurt, but it did. If you didn't say it, it might cease to be. You hated the sluggishness most, tried to ignore it. The doctor told you fatigue was normal, but you tried coffee and Diet Coke, tried changing your diet. Exercises, too, but they were tougher than you thought, and when your joints swelled enough, nearly impossible.

You bought a membership to a facility with a warm-water pool and took classes for people with joint issues. You were the youngest in class by about forty years. A former marine befriended you. He had grandchildren not much younger than you. He was completely bald. Your bob had grown out to your shoulders, but not more. In your warm-water exercise classes, you clipped your hair on your head, not in a bun, of course, but so it wouldn't get saturated with chlorine.

The former marine liked working out with you because he thought you were serious. You were. Using a noodle wrapped around your torso for buoyancy, you scissored your legs, or pedaled an imaginary bike. There were many ladies in the class.

"They talk too much, aren't here to work out," the former marine grumbled. The pool area was filled with the cluck and clatter of chatting and the splashing of the exercises.

The workouts were not strenuous, but you felt better. You had more energy for work. You worked in marketing, had a knack for writing press releases that resulted in articles, and advertising copy that got attention. Not bad work, but you craved something more creative. You liked being able to pay your bills, for your warm-water workouts. You went to the workouts five days a week after work, sometimes on Saturday mornings.

Some Saturdays, however, you slept in. You never felt like you got enough rest, but you tried to keep up appearances.

When did you start to dream about dancing? You went to writers' workshops for long weekends. You called these vacations. Occasionally you wrote about dancers, and the faculty at these workshops encouraged you to write more. At night, head on pillow, you dreamed in white, lines of tutus in *Giselle* and *La Bayadère*. The white of Balanchine's *Symphony in C*. You kept up with writers of dance criticism, read about Darci Kistler in her husband's version of *Swan Lake*. More white.

The white in your world flashed hot in your joints, but you didn't complain. You tried not to think about it. You got shots, procedures. You kept up with the warm-water workouts. Your right knee was always swollen. Joints usually swell systemically, both sides, but your right knee was always worse than your left.

When you danced, your strongest side was always left.

You attempted to hide the swelling by covering your legs. No shorts. Skirts to mid-calf, your favorite. Pants, too. Your legs lightened several shades paler than the rest of your skin; you continued to hide beneath clothes. Legs never in the sun. Your limp became a harder aspect to disguise, your gate a hobble. You kept a sunny disposition, made jokes about being a gimp.

Stairs became arch enemy number one. Climbing up or down turned out to be difficult, slow. You hid nothing but didn't talk about it. Really, what was there to say?

When you started writing in earnest about dancing, you grew out your hair. When others read your work, they looked at you, assessed what they saw. "You still have the look of a dancer," they told you.

You know it was the hair—length a hallmark for ballet dancers. Your body, not large, morphed into a softer, doughier version, no longer sleek and angular. You didn't think you looked like a dancer at all, and it made you unhappy. You no longer had the duck walk, the way a dancer couldn't help but hold her turnout. You didn't feel toned, muscles gone slack. You tried sitting up straight in your chair, trying to preserve your posture.

You still had a long neck, of course. That didn't change over the years. Maybe that gave you the look that others found dancer-like. Maybe they were looking for whatever signs they could find.

Your legs felt lumpy and useless, your arms a thin spindle of nothing. Knuckles swollen, too.

When you wrote about dance, a part of you was freed. You remembered the bourrées from *Raymonda*'s third act variation, the happy petit allegro of Peasant Pas from *Giselle*. Trying to capture it on paper frustrated you in a good way. When you tried to explain this to others, they looked at you like you had a third eye, or a giant pimple on the tip of your nose.

You wrote leaps, *little bits of flying*. Closed your eyes, remembered the feeling. You could hear the instructions from your teacher. "You should be able to clap your hands under your legs when you leap." You were once a firecracker girl.

You returned to the writers' workshop, got more encouragement. A somewhat famous writer liked your material. "The bad news is that this is probably a novel," he said over drinks with the rest of your workshop group.

You didn't tell him that the only way to deal with your grief was to write the world you used to know. Instead, you let yourself be happy that something worked. Alone, you considered this question: why fiction? The facts of your life still hurt. The knee was still swollen tight, walking slow, labored, often with a cane. On the page, you created characters who did *Don Quixote* leaps. Ink-on-paper legs were strong, extended, lean. Your narration curled around your characters, dancers, like soutenu turns. In your actual life, your body tried to curl around your failing legs.

The only things to do: live with the disease, enroll in a writing program. You did both, hobbling around a mountainous campus with your cane keeping you upright. You taught and attended classes, what writing grad students do. Most of the time, you felt happy, especially writing, focusing on writing, those things that released you from your body. Your hair reached down your back; your writing focused on the lives of dancers. Physically, your body continued degenerating, but your mind took flight the way your legs used to. Most days, this was enough to sustain you.

For the first time, you wrote about your own experience as a dancer. It exhausted you. It pleased you. It got published, to your shock and delight. Mostly, you retreated into characters, let them dance the way you longed to.

The director of dance at the university where you studied writing read your published piece. Reading the piece, it was clear you'd had training. A modern dancer by trade, she asked you to coach a student with a ballet background, to teach her a classical variation. You had not been in a studio in over a decade, nearly two. You agreed anyway.

The smell of the studio was familiar—the sweat of work hung heavy, despite opened windows, despite cleaning. Dance studios smelled of human effort.

It's not like you to complain about pain. Suck it up, you told yourself. As a dancer, you ached too, different than this ache. That was the ache of exertion. When it got bad enough, hurt too much to walk, you called your rheumatologist. X-rays showed you both the culprit: your right knee no longer had any cartilage. Imagine clack of bones knitting together.

"I don't know how you're even getting around," your rheumatologist said. It didn't make you feel like less of a wimp.

After surgery, your wound had to heal before you could

shower. Your mother washed your hair in the sink. Clean hair became your guilty pleasure. You worked out the tangles with a comb; your conditioner made your hair smell like kiwi fruit.

A week after surgery, you returned to the dance studio. Perched on a stool, you taught ballet class. You relied solely on your voice, your ability to articulate the combinations and corrections. After every few exercises at the barre, you asked the dancers to rotate so you could see and instruct them all. It was as if your class was a conveyor belt of ballet dancers. They willingly complied. Your friends and family thought you were nuts, but it felt right to get to work. More and more you had been asked to teach dance, and to your surprise, you found that you were good at it.

You still wrote daily, mostly about dancing.

Once into it, you ended up loving physical therapy. Like the early days of your dance training, you gained a sense of accomplishment. You learned to walk properly again, no limp. Your orthopedic surgeon was pleased with the results.

Your physical therapist had you do basic exercises on a Pilates reformer. You loved this part of therapy because as a dancer, you also did Pilates. Plié was as natural as breath. Your PT was thrilled, more flexion. Not perfect, but better.

Could you ever dance again? This was the question always on your mind. You didn't ask. You knew better than to think you'd ever dance like you once did, but you dared to hope all the same.

Sometimes you flirt with cutting your hair, but you don't. You're in the studio several days a week now. You walk well; you can demonstrate simple things. You feel your arms and upper body, what used to be your expressive port de bras. You develop muscles in your back again.

You still swell inside your body, but your medicine is helping more. You still get tired, fatigued, but find inner velocity that pushes you forward. You remember what your physical therapist told you. "The people who tend to have it the worst complain the least," she said. "Don't ever let this get the better of you."

Sometimes you still get told you look like a dancer. No one has ever told you that you look like a writer. Most times, people comment on your transformation: no walker, no cane, no limp. Darci Kistler, a former idol, retires from dancing. You start coaching private students, and they start going to summer intensives. Most days, you write and experience dance. You are always busy with both. You take weekly shots to keep going. Most of the time, you don't mind. There's not a lot of time for what could have been.

Sometimes you wear your hair twisted in a high bun, other times you braid a long length of ponytail into a thick rope. Sometimes you leave it long and wild. You keep brushes in your car and bag. You condition it to keep it healthy and shiny. Trim the split ends. At night, you comb your long brown hair, now with stands of gray and sometimes pure white.

In Sickness

THE WORST POSSIBLE THING HAPPENED. It's what you most want to know and it is what I least want to tell you. Why is it that we must tell that silent, horrible thing? And how can I tell you, without being the object of pity? When you are the main character of your own story, the process of sifting through what you want to tell and what you're willing to tell competes with what is expected of you to tell. If I tell you I was a ballet dancer, it might pique your interest, but if I tell you I was a dancer turned rheumatoid arthritis patient, there's something more there you want to read. I know it. I'm always told, "That's what you should write about."

As a dancer sidelined by rheumatoid arthritis at the age of twenty-one, I often feel it is the RA, the uncontrollable disease that makes my story interesting, and that makes me feel cheap. It's a tough truth to consider: that I'm just not that interesting without the RA. Sure, I was never a famous dancer. Like many young girls, I gave a big chunk of my life to training, only to be suitable for pretty lowly work, a member of the corps. All I wanted was to dance. It didn't matter to me that I wasn't a star, so long as I could be a dancer. The word still holds promise for me, that fairy-tale creature my imagination conjured up in my youth. I tasted what it would be like to be her, and I'd be lying if I said I don't enjoy telling those stories, even if they're ordinary. Lurking around the corner, though, is the RA. I feel like being diagnosed with RA makes people pay attention to my story. What's depressing is it happens to be the same thing I hate most of all about who I am. That's where the drama is, others assure me. But I know the truth. It's just an auto-immune disease. It doesn't make me special, it just makes me sick.

More than anything, I don't want to be sick.

What upsets me most about writing "the RA story" is the idea that it might sound like I'm looking for pity. I'm not looking for anyone to feel sorry for me, not interested in pulling on anyone's heartstrings. In fact, I'm pretty sure that's part of why I don't want to write about the RA. I don't want to manufacture a version of me that dwells in the disease, mythologizes it, and gives it power through the written word.

Still, I suspect it is what you want to know.

Once, someone asked me to write about my sense of dread, as if I could feel the RA coming upon me. The question of dread lingered like a thought bubble following me around. The problem with coming at it this way is that it's false. RA isn't about a growing dread—its timeline is different. It is a disease that often just shows up and manifests itself in quick, devastating blowups. For me, the disease didn't build. From the time I first showed symptoms to my diagnosis was just a few short months—nothing, within the span of a lifetime. It wasn't dread that I felt, rather it was like when my computer automatically shuts down for reasons I can't explain. One day, it just happened and then I scrambled. My body sort of broke down from the inside out. I played catch-up, figuring out what to do because of this reboot. There wasn't much time for dread.

The first time I knew something was wrong, I felt it in my spine. I woke one morning to find that I couldn't hold my body upright. Unable to work out the kinks through stretching, I went to a sports medicine specialist. He was a tall, athletic doctor in a crisp white lab coat. My appointment felt like a normal doctor's visit—the usual procedures, like listening to my heart and checking my reflexes. It escalated; X-rays, which didn't show much of anything. When I went to see the doctor about my first ailment, my back, he suspected the discomfort was caused by stress fractures. Not accustomed to major injuries, I was a little shocked. Even though I took good care of myself, this diagnosis wasn't beyond what I thought could be normal. I put my body through its paces six days a week, day-in, day-out dancing. The stress and strain, I thought, was catching up with me. This had happened to other dancers, and many returned after therapy and a short recovery period. I believed in my youth and figured, with some care, I'd bounce back. My doctor agreed—a few weeks' rest and I should be feeling back to normal.

I knew there was more to these "injuries" when those few weeks passed and my back still hurt, and then my knees started to swell, and other joints ached. It didn't seem right because I had been sitting out, resting. The results were frustrating. During a follow-up visit, the sports medicine specialist prescribed Daypro, an anti-inflammatory, and it helped for a time, until, of course, it didn't. I'd swell up again. The more I sat in those white-walled offices that smelled of heavy-duty disinfectant, the more it dawned on me that whatever was going on with these so-called injuries, something more significant was happening to me. But I couldn't quite come to terms with the idea that my body wouldn't hold up. There was no diagnosis to support my suspicions that these effects were long-term.

When I thought I was ready to return, ballet classes fatigued me. I used to love the petit allegro, a string of light jumps strung together, bouncy and happy, but by that part of class I was lucky if I was still upright and moving. Sidelined, I watched other dancers rehearse ballets I thought I would be dancing. And while I watched, acting as though I would soon be back in the ranks, I physically didn't progress past my "injuries." Something was very wrong, and my body knew—sent out the signals before I could even begin to comprehend what was happening.

I struggled through a few months of trying to dance before I knew—I just knew—these problems were much worse than anyone thought. The sports medicine doctor told me that I might not have the endurance for dance. As if it could be that simple. At the time, this wasn't enough reason to abandon ballet. The thought of not dancing felt unfathomable. I'd never considered a future that didn't include dance. I found ways to make myself useful. I did light repairs to costumes, but even threading a needle was harder than it had been before. I'd chastise myself for acting ungrateful, for not sucking up my bad luck and waiting it out.

Still, at the end of the season, I didn't go back. Everything hurt too much. I'd take a temporary break, I reasoned, and find a new doctor, or work with a physical therapist, and return stronger than ever. If there wasn't dread, there was doubt. I still didn't know exactly what was going on with my body. I couldn't ignore that I felt different and that it wasn't something I could wish away or work to fix. It wasn't like ballet was a hobby for me, and it seemed that performing would be gone almost as soon as it had begun. I just couldn't accept what went wrong.

Most times, when I make a change, the only thing I can do is focus on that change itself. Like a horse with blinders, I see only straight ahead, and maybe this blinkered self knows better than the rest of me what has to be done, how to keep me from getting spooked. I focus on what needs to be done, not what's left behind. Did I know I was leaving performing? Maybe subconsciously I did know. What I figured out was not what to do with the rest of my life, but what to do the next Monday, the Monday after that, maybe the next month. I kept my mind on the short term, leaving enough space open to hope for what could be. Miracles sometimes happen, I told myself, even though I didn't really believe it. In the meantime, I was happy to follow other paths because, who knew, maybe one day I'd wake up feeling better and would slip back into my life of dance.

While my body continued to wage a silent, interior war on itself, I didn't talk about what was happening to me, not to my family or friends. I tucked away my feelings, the same way I'm keeping you at arm's length. I even tried to ignore the symptoms. I had to separate myself from the truth of my situation. Perhaps this was weak, a way of not facing the facts, but any other approach would have been too devastating. I adapted to the new situation by never fully giving up on the old.

During this time, I went to college, learned that I couldn't really be wholly unhappy as the slanted afternoon sunlight filtered through the persimmon and crimson leaves and cast itself along the gray surface of Indiana limestone. The crisp autumn air made it easy to breathe, and walking outside between classes to the library became a way to deal with the fact that I was no longer dancing; I shelved that old idea of being a dancer, leaving it in a remote dark corner of my psyche, like a box in the attic or basement gathering dust, full of cast-off clothes and knickknacks I wasn't ready to get rid of. Rather than dwell, I became preoccupied with other concerns: reading novels, writing papers, lab work, and exams. All the stuff of school. Then no one could accuse me of feeling sorry for myself—least of all, me. Pity parties aren't my thing.

College did open me up. I liked learning about new subjects—everything from freshman psych to Victorian lit— but nothing appealed to me so much as writing. I'd always kept journals, and so I happily lost myself in the world of the imagination, rather than focusing on what was happening to my body. I wrote other lives, escaping the one I lived.

In school, to get by physically meant literally placing one foot in front of the other. At this point, I could still hide the fact that my body didn't work quite right. I was stiff and sore, even though I wasn't working out all that much, but I shoved it out of mind, cracking open the books and getting lost in the literary. No one else could see that I was losing control over my body. Not yet.

Maybe there is no escaping fate. That's RA—it's a fate, not a choice. Before I knew I was in the grip of a disease, before I knew its name and its ways, I discounted the symptoms. I wasn't dancing anymore, so I shouldn't feel lousy. But of course there were lousy days, many of them, and then, like a parting of the clouds, there were good days. As distraction, I made friends and went to parties and dated boys and tried to be "normal." Sometimes, when alone, I thought about ballet, missing the daily routine of dance class, but before the tears came, I would call a friend or rent a movie or open a book. My only cure was to do something, to take small actions that allowed me to ignore the truth: I was not dancing. I still hoped for a return, of course. I lived in bliss between what could have been and what might be.

Only when my knees swelled so much that it was painful to walk, painful to sit, painful to lie down, I finally sought help. When the swelling was something I couldn't hide, I had to do something. What I didn't know until one October night when I finally drove to an urgent care facility for relief was that I was going to be led by RA. I would have to try to understand that my body had been hard at work destroying itself, and that there wasn't a thing I could do about it until I asked for help. Even then, help would be imperfect. That night, the physician at the urgent care facility told me I needed to see a specialist. The swelling was bad and indicative of something else. I was given more anti-inflammatories and a referral to a rheumatologist. When I final saw this specialist, he took my blood and ran it though the tests that would confirm that I tested positive for the rheumatoid factor. I faced these doctors and my diagnosis alone.

Truth is a tough teacher. My truth: I couldn't escape RA. No one can do anything to avoid getting it. Researchers of the disease know there's a trigger for people predisposed to it, but there's no test right now to say whether my genetic make-up makes me vulnerable or not, until I got it, and then, well, I was in it.

Gold salts, Daypro, Celebrex, Azulfidine, Enbrel. When you're a chronic disease patient, the list of past and present medications becomes a terrible little chemical parade. I need them and curse them. What bothers me about medication is the idea of being dependent. And despite the therapies I've tried through the years, my body still finds ways to ravage me under the skin. My body had never been perfect. I'd worked hard to make it into a dancer's body. The mother of a boy I knew once told me I had shapely legs. At the time, I blushed, especially at the word "shapely," which seemed to me so old-fashioned. I was proud of the compliment, though. I no longer had those shapely legs, ones made of hard-earned toil and long, lithe muscle. My body hadn't always willingly conformed to a dancer's figure, but I'd shaped myself through technique, good eating habits, Pilates, and determination. Now my body truly was an enemy, not something I might, through training and self-discipline, conquer. After my diagnosis, I accepted that I was sick, only in so much as I might try to put up a defense against it. This second stage of decline happened slowly, a jag of bad days, limpy, swelly, achy days, followed by better ones, but never, ever days where I felt fully healthy. Over time, I took on the daily hurting until I didn't quite notice how pain affected me anymore.

Or maybe I didn't want to notice. So much of how I have dealt with RA's blows has been to ignore what I've lost, how I continue to slip physically. Even when the injections changed from the old-fashioned gold salts to the newfangled Enbrel, from something administered in the doctor's office to something I gave myself at home, I wanted to believe I could be better again. I wanted to believe that I would overcome it, that I wouldn't have to take anti-inflammatories daily to try to make my body behave. Maybe I even thought, beyond hope, that I could be a dancer again, my body in service to beauty, that elusive ideal.

Instead, RA continued attacking my joints, despite my efforts, literally eating away my cartilage, in some cases, until my joints were disfigured, and until all the healthy connective tissue was gone. I could only do what I was doing, but what happens when that's not enough? I had no answer, save the cane I acquired to help me walk.

I have to wonder, is this really what you want to know? Think about it. If you read this series of events—that I went from not dancing, to not walking well, to needing a cane, to needing a walker—perhaps you'll feel better. Maybe you have problems in your life, but you have your health. You might even feel sorry for me. At least I never had to deal with that, you think. This is a pessimistic view, and it haunts me. I don't want you to think of me as a diseased person. No *poor girl whose dream was snatched away*. It feels cheap, and yet, here I am telling it.

Perhaps I should think better of you. Perhaps I should consider that you want to see me come out okay, and that this is just where I battle my personal villain. That's the more hopeful view, I suppose. Perhaps too hopeful.

What are we, together, trying to gain by this exercise?

When writers write our true stories, we're told there is a contract with you, the reader. That contract seems very one-sided. Tell the whole truth, but make it worthwhile. Don't make it up, but make it dramatic and poignant. Even better if you can work in the Little Engine That Could myth—get knocked down and get back up. In the meantime, give us the gritty, terrible details.

Here I am, putting it to paper. I have to admit, I'm a little ashamed. I promised myself not to use my RA to gain attention, not to let it become a defining attribute of who I am. If I try to show you this side of me, this side I barely even let myself acknowledge, I wonder is there a reward? In return for this confession, will you also accept my joy, small and personal as it is? Could you also love me in health?

The blue hanging placard in my car signified a major defeat, because it officially branded me as a disabled person. No ballerina had been physically handicapped as I now was. Alicia Alonso had danced even when she became legally blind, but her limbs still worked. I, however, ceased to work right. The placard arrived at a time when I required it. Most days, walking was slow and labored, and I needed to be closer to buildings and such just to function on a basic level. So, officially, I became disabled. Maybe my ego couldn't take it, or maybe denial is just that strong, but I hated the whole idea of being disabled and never fully appreciated that the placard and proximity were meant to help me. In my mind this was the antithesis of being a dancer, and even after what I'd been through there was that thread that refused to snap clean and allow me to think of myself as something else.

Of course, I didn't discuss it. If, when I was out with friends, they walked faster than I did, I just tried to catch up, but I never asked them to slow down. I didn't ask people to help me carry things or do things for me if I didn't have to. I hardly asked for help with opening bottles and jars, even though my wrists were thick with hot fluid and refused to twist. Pride stood in the way of those requests. If I was tired, there was coffee, and if I hurt, I felt it was my job to suck it up. No one would want to be around a person who pitied herself. More importantly, I wouldn't accept such behavior from myself. If I didn't talk about it, maybe no one else would, and everyone, including me, could forget that I limped around, half-useless. That's the best explanation I have for why I refused to acknowledge my steady decline.

It's probably also a big part of the reason I've resisted writing about it.

I remember the day I realized I'd gone a decade as an RA patient. Other things, good things, during this time, had happened, too. I'd finished college and worked in marketing with some professional success. I'd gotten married. These few things made me feel like a pretty normal person. As I lived with RA, I'd put together a different kind of life than the one I'd imagined. So, when a new coworker had asked me how long I'd had RA, and when I counted the years and figured out it was more than ten, I wanted to burst into tears. But I don't cry in front of people. Later, alone, the tears came. By the next day, I'd tucked the whole incident away. Time passed. My husband and I bought our first house and rescued a beagle, and I focused on these good things.

What persisted, though, was an old ache, and not a physical one. An autoimmune disease makes you feel trapped by your body. Nothing works like it should. I often thought about my youth, about studying to be a ballet dancer. Sometimes, in the kitchen, I'd try to do simple things, but I couldn't. RA had taken that from me. Forget plié. Forget ballet posture, erect, with stomach pulled in and shoulders down, the long, strong back. Grand jété— little bits of flying—a thing of the past. If you complain about it, the disease wins. That's how I felt—pity was for the self-indulgent, not for me. Even if I wouldn't feel sorry for myself, I had to accept that living with RA was much different than the life I'd once hoped for. But forgetting was hard, especially when inside me there was that piece that didn't want to forget. Once I had danced and had loved it.

Then came the time when I made dancers on paper. It finally happened when I thought about applying to graduate school for writing, when I started to get excited about doing something with my life that gave me creative and personal expression. Sure, my limbs were anchored, but my mind, I hoped, could still reach and twist and soar. People choose to do MFA programs in creative writing for many reasons, and at the heart of my decision was the idea of recreating dance as word pictures, to keep it alive for me in some new way. I didn't want the dancer inside me to wither. I wasn't quite a writer—a part of me felt like a battered old ballet dancer hiding out among writers. Still, I kept putting the language of movement on paper, its own satisfaction.

Writing about dance is difficult because dance resides so much in the body that it often resists words. I remembered, though, as I created characters to dance for me, the action verbs my beloved teacher, Mrs. Gooden, used: resist, stretch, release, bend, lift, gather, coil, reach, suspend. Dance lives through action verbs, which happen to also be the building blocks of good writing. Even though I was physically muted and stationary, the words cracked open that world of movement. I wrote mostly fiction at first, and I found my characters aching for the beauty that ballet enabled, my ideal.

A common adage about writing is that it is a process of discovery. Perhaps all art is. For me, writing became the vehicle for rediscovering how much I had loved dancing, and how much I still loved it, even though my physical being completely rejected it. Dance had made me as much as anything else had, and I loved it completely, even as my body cast away all things physical, all the elements of a dancer's body. I could hope for better for those dancers I created in my imagination, who took form on paper in ink.

The more I wrote, the more my body declined. One really had nothing to do with the other, but the irony isn't lost on me. I've read about other dancers leaving ballet, and their difficulties are, at once, both similar to and different from my own. My childhood idol, Gelsey Kirkland, wrote about her addiction to cocaine and how her obsession with perfection through dance drove her to desperate conditions. She was once considered the greatest ballerina of her age and, to me, one of the most beautiful. A part of me wants to preserve her as that standard of beauty. The childlike glow that ballet ignited in me has never fully been tamped down, and I often think that I've never shed my identity as a dancer because even though my career was just a flicker, it lit a larger flame. A part of me will always be that young girl, searching for the promise of beauty only ballet seemed to offer, and when I lose that, I'll lose a big part of myself to a more cynical version.

I'm not wholly sure why I equate ballet and beauty, but I do, and so perhaps, too, I want to cling to the idea that I could be beautiful. It's such a common desire, I'm almost ashamed to admit it. Fact is, I'm not particularly pretty, but mismatched—pale skin and blue-gray eyes, but with dark hair. My head seems too big for my body, and my heart-shaped face has always looked pudgy, even when I was slender. I have a giant forehead that unfurls the way Antarctica does on a flat map—the great uninteresting plane of my face. My lower lip is bigger than the upper, giving me a crooked smile and perpetual pout. My skin rebels in little outbreaks of acne. The muscles in my legs, which used to be strong, are punchier, rounder than I'd like, and my torso a little too long for the rest of my proportions. I have a butt, too much rump for a ballerina, and hips, but when I was dancing and thinner, I was flat-chested, and so I looked lopsided and a bit pear-shaped.

My hands, though, used to be lovely—delicate with long fingers. Smooth, unwrinkled skin. I even had naturally pretty fingernails that looked as if I had them French manicured. My hands are a great casualty of RA, showing the effects of swelling and inner deterioration. They've become knobbier with thick fingers and swollen knuckles. But once I had the hands of a ballerina, and even I liked how they looked.

Imagine, once you had performed splits in midair. Now, sitting in a doctor's office chair, you're shown an X-ray that confirms you no longer have any cartilage in your right knee. For years, you've hobbled around with the aid of a cane, but now even that's not an option. You have two choices. You either have a total knee replacement or you figure out how to get around with a walker or wheelchair.

You are thirty-six years old.

One of the few times I've cried in public was that day in my rheumatologist's office. I guess it wasn't so public, but it wasn't alone. I hate that I broke down like that, but finally I couldn't keep my composure. My rheumatologist is a kind man, with a no-nonsense way about talking about RA. The choices were limited, and I had to accept that. I already had, of course. By this time, putting weight on my leg was more pain than I could hide, and relying on a cane was not enough. I could barely walk, but I did, perhaps by sheer willpower, to get from one place to another.

Instead of telling me not to cry, my rheumatologist let the sobs flow, until there was a break, and then he brought me into his business office and called the orthopedic surgeon he thought was the best in town. He took such a personal interest in making sure I was going to do this thing I didn't want to do. I think he knew I'd already decided to have the knee replacement surgery, but both my rheumatologist and the orthopedist gave me the option of calling back with a decision. I slept on it, but I didn't toss or turn a bit. I knew I had to get the surgery, so first thing in the morning, I called and asked for the next available appointment. Once I made the decision, I was determined to get it done as soon as possible. No waiting around or mulling it over. Once again, I moved on quickly.

Though I was able to get in for surgery within a couple of weeks, I still needed a way to get around in the meantime, and so I found myself in a medical supply store, shopping for a walker. I wanted something basic, because I was hoping that I wouldn't need it all that much—just pre- and post-op. Strangely, this view betrayed optimism I hadn't dared to feel in a long time.

There were two elderly ladies in the store with me. One checked out a high-end walker with wheels and hand brakes like a bike. The salesperson had tried talking me into a similar model, but I wanted the cheaper one, without wheels, without bells and whistles. Basic worked for me. It seemed weird to think of walkers as having bells and whistles, but they do. The other elderly lady in the store bought a walker organizer—a fabric caddy with various pockets—that fits over the bar across the front of the walker so you can keep things like keys and cell phones handy. The lady suggested I also get a walker organizer. She showed me the fancy ones made of zebra-, cheetah-, and leopard-print fabrics.

I decided right there I would just use a backpack or my pockets. It was too much for me to consider a cheetah-print walker organizer. It certainly didn't seem fashion forward, and I'd only just accepted the need for the walker. I was not ready to give in to accessorizing, making the apparatus into a statement, not even when the salesperson asked if I might also like the see the giraffe print.

Before my surgery, my mother came to stay with me to help with the day-to-day stuff around my house. She cooked, cleaned, and drove me to appointments. My father also came for regular visits, both to be with my mom, who he missed at home, and me, as I prepared for surgery. During one of these visits, Dad went to see the orthopedist with me. He always carried a small notebook and a maroon Montblanc pen, and he took notes on what I needed to do and what I could expect, all of the details that only partially sunk in as I sat in the white examination room trying to be brave, or at least to not look nervous.

When my father asked the doctor what I would not ask—what were the chances of success?—the orthopedist told him he would do his best, but certain things were for God to decide. He did say he thought I would be free of pain, but there had been a lot of damage. He explained that many patients could do much more after surgery than before, and in spite of all the hope that had quietly slipped away over the years, I felt like maybe things would get better. Maybe I had to feel this way so that I didn't feel like a thirty-six-year-old getting a surgery usually meant for a senior citizen. And so I could believe it was, in fact, the best choice.

At this point, perhaps you're thinking, yes, the happy ending is coming. This might make you sigh with relief, or become disenchanted with the story, feeling the happy ending wasn't earned. There's some judgment at the prospect of happiness, just as this entire story opens me up for scrutiny. Even though the surgery would help with the pain I had in my right knee, even though it partially restored what had been destroyed, it did not, of course, cure my RA. I never thought it would, and you shouldn't think that either. I still have swelling, fatigue, fever, aches, joint damage. I can also get around in a fairly normal way now.

Happy is a relative state.

The night after my surgery I got very little sleep because I had intense pain. The night nurse had already threatened to catheterize me if I didn't urinate, and so I willed myself to pee, only to be left atop a full bedpan. So things didn't start off great that evening, and once the meds wore off, I felt like my thigh muscle was being slowly shredded with a cheese grater. My dad stood vigil by my bedside, getting only sporadic sleep in an easy chair. Luckily, I didn't have to share a room with another patient. My father tried desperately to get the nurse to give me something for the pain, and perhaps she did, but I honestly can't remember. I remember him holding my hand so maybe I wouldn't feel so alone, and I remember squeezing because it hurt that bad.

Dancers build muscle memory from the day-in, day-out study of technique. Over the years, my thigh muscle had learned a new muscle memory, trying to pull my kneecap up from my deteriorating joint. My orthopedic surgeon told me that even under full anesthesia my thigh muscle would not relax at first—the only time he'd ever seen this. The muscle still tried to manipulate the kneecap to avoid painful grinding in the joint. The body's ability to adapt to protect itself is quite remarkable in this way. Though my orthopedist finally did get it to relax, my muscles retained a dancer's memory. What could have been a minor curiosity signified to me a small connection to my former self.

After the first night, things did get better, but it was slow going. My leg was strapped into a machine that helped stimulate the new joint by continually keeping it in motion, as if pedaling or walking. I could lie down as this happened or sit propped on pillows, and many times I'd get calls from friends, which were welcome distractions, as the machine churned my leg. I learned exercises I would have to perform daily and made arrangements for physical therapy. When I was released from the hospital, I was given strong pain pills, but within a few days, I stopped taking them because I wasn't hurting so much, not compared to how much I'd hurt before the surgery, and I worried about becoming dependent on them. Pain, by then, was one thing I knew how to contend with.

In the weeks immediately following my surgery, I still needed the walker. My wound needed to heal, and I had to learn to walk again. I'd limped for so long, accommodating a joint that continued to fall apart, that my legs literally needed retraining on how to correctly put one foot in front of the other.

Dance had taught me how to train. So even though it took three physical therapists and some unconventional approaches, like a Pilates reformer and manipulation of the joint under anesthesia by my orthopedic surgeon, I finally made progress. First, though, a remarkable thing happened. As the wound from the surgery healed, I stopped hurting for the first time in what felt like forever. I felt nothing, and it was bliss. My father said he watched my facial features loosen and soften, too. He said I looked younger because I no longer carried the pain on my face. I didn't know it was so evident. Perhaps I'd never hidden my anguish at all, that it was there, on display, the whole time.

I've never regained full mobility with my prosthetic knee, but I'm able to do things now I thought I might never do again. Take the good with bad, the saying goes, or is it the other way around? The ending isn't simply happy or sad. It isn't really an ending.

This past June I had the opportunity to renew my handicap placard for my car. But as the date for this renewal came and slipped by, I've yet to have my doctor sign the papers I'd need to file at the DMV. I can walk from any space in the lot to where I need to go. I can walk without the aid of a cane. I can walk at a normal pace and move with relative ease.

Once a week I slip the needle of a prefilled syringe into the fleshier parts of me, dispensing medicinal liquid that helps to balance my whacked-out immune system. During the week, I spend several hours in a studio, in the presence of dancers as their teacher. Twice a day, anti-inflammatories. All this give and take, but I've found an uneasy peace.

I've given you a version of my story, the best I have to give. I crafted it with words I chose and plucked so carefully, shaped through revision. I've given you this tale and you will decide what to make of it, what to make of me. I have no control over that. You may judge or feel or discount. Perhaps a concoction of all three. I accept that, once written, my story is no longer wholly mine. Still, I give it to you.

Today I am sick, and tomorrow I will be sick, as I will be every day until I die. I may not like it, but that's how it is. The rest of my life will always be entwined with rheumatoid arthritis. But it's my choice to also be something more, to not feel sick, to still find those shadows of a dancer, which is to say tiny flecks of magic, within me. Like anyone who is hopelessly in love, I will always be the keeper of a flame.

A Royal in Appalachia

THOUGH IT WAS ONLY NOON, we cleaned the flutes and Mr. Peter Franklin-White poured champagne. My student Megan, a dance minor at WVU, had finished cataloging a box of ballet artifacts to be sent to the New York Public Library for the Performing Arts, part of her independent study project in Dance History, and I was the lucky instructor tasked with overseeing her work. If champagne seemed like overkill for a job well done, you have to know Peter.

Peter, a British-born dancer, regaled us with a story from his company days, of "a minor nobleman of major means" who invited the Royal Ballet Company to his castle. The host, a patron of the company, decided to serve every member champagne. "It's what you do in a castle," the host had told Peter. And though Peter's house is no castle, it is filled with unlikely treasures. From his basement, outfitted as a makeshift wine cellar, he appeared with a bottle, a spring in his step, which at ninety years old, is quite a feat.

In a house on top of a hillside in the First Ward neighborhood of Morgantown, West Virginia, Megan and I toasted friendship with Peter. I also live in First Ward, in a little house on a gentle slope, downhill from where Peter's house looks out over the neighborhood. I had once danced, too, but never with a company as lofty as the Royal. Queen Elizabeth was never "my boss," and my treasures are only of personal importance.

Peter lifted his flute into a ray of light cast through a small window, watched it bubble up like laughter made visible, and then he brought the flute to his lips and sipped. Megan and I followed suit, the champagne dry and ticklish in the mouth but satisfying in that way that good drink is.

"I only drink champagne with friends," he said. I find this to be quite right. I watched Peter sit and sip, and despite his advanced age, I could see, by his fluid gesture in raising the flute and his easy yet erect posture in the chair, those shadows of the principal character dancer he once was. Behind him hung a commemorative program, a framed bit of creamy silk, edged in gold tassels, with gala's offerings: second act *Swan Lake* and the whole of *The Firebird*. For me, Peter's treasures were the stuff of biographies and documentaries. For Peter, they all pointed to stories, as much as drinking champagne in a castle, as any royal would do.

To be a former dancer is a precarious thing because I'm not really sure what to do with myself. Teach? Write about dancing? Become something else? These questions linger and haunt, tease and taunt, and I'm left with the careful wreckage of what used to be a dancer's body. I find myself trying on different roles—not unlike learning variations from different ballets—trying to figure out which one suits me. They all do and don't. And while I had many role

models on stage, ballerinas I still too easily mythologize,
I don't have many role models on how not to be on stage.

Perhaps I should be looking toward my old teachers, those
who performed and retired and taught me and hundreds
of other girls the ropes of plié, tendu, dégagé. But I find
that my teachers stay tucked in that part of my imagination
left to memory. I find myself preserving and mythologiz-
ing them, just as I do the ballerinas, the stars of my youth.
Nostalgia, that pretty place, often rebuffs critical assess-
ment, like the thorns and vines and leaves that surround
Aurora's castle in *The Sleeping Beauty*. And while I'm not
relegated to a hundred years of sleep, waiting for a prince
to kiss me, waking the slumber of dance and movement
from my limbs, I still feel caught in ballet's fairy-tale place,
wanting to preserve that sense of magic that drew me to it
when I was young.

I don't know how to be in the here and now—middle-
aged, sidelined by a chronic disease, teaching some and
writing some, and sometimes just being a wife or friend or
daughter, nothing at all to do with dance or art. How does
one live as an ex-dancer?

"I lost my hearing in the Blitz," Peter told us. Living in
London during the war, Peter danced with Sadler's Wells,
the predecessor of the Royal Ballet. He lived in the theater,
danced despite the bombs, when London refused to kowtow
to Hitler's barrage.

Picture an eerie December day, too warm for holidays,
but with a grayness that Peter called a "half-night day."
Assembled in the small but comfortable dining room, we
were all former dancers. Peter and I were nearly the same
height. I'm five foot five, no longer the whittled girl of my
dancing days, but slender, my long brown hair flecked with

strands of gray. Still, dancer hair, which could be coiled neatly into a bun. Peter's hair was full and white. We supported ourselves upright in the chairs with back muscles that had been worked as part of a dancer's posture. Perhaps we showed leftovers from a life in dance—the fluidity in which Peter gestured to a picture, his easy, graceful stride, or even the way I tilted my head, gently craning my long neck, a feature once praised by even my harshest teachers, as if I could have willed myself into producing it.

That day the stage was Peter's, though, and as dancers we understood how rank and file works, the hierarchy particular to dance. He was principal and I was, as I often had been, the girl in the corps.

I visited Peter often, stopping in as the winter slumped into spring. On one particular visit, in his kitchen, Peter instructed me to sit on a high, stool-like chair, as he went about the preparations. Water heated to "nearly boiling." A pot warmed in the ancient microwave. Peter kept his tea, Earl Grey loose leaf, in the freezer, neatly wrapped and placed inside a Ziploc bag. He scooped a generous portion—three heaping tablespoons—and dropped it into the pot. He poured the water, once ready, in the teapot from an electric kettle. Then he covered it with a cozy.

"It must stay at least three minutes," Peter said. The directions are as precise as any combination or corrections in a ballet class. Dancers are creatures of peculiar habits, even with nondance activities, even, perhaps especially, tea. I had to wonder, would there be a test on how to make proper British tea?

Peter's movements were slow and deliberate. To serve the tea, he used a strainer over the cup so there were no stray leaves. Opening his yellow fridge, he asked if I would care for a splash of milk. Afraid of getting it wrong, I asked if that's the way tea is supposed to be served. Peter shrugged. He said milk or sugar was personal preference.

"My father drinks tea with milk," I said. "So that's how I'll take it."

"Your father has an English background?" he asked as he pulled a carton of milk from the fridge.

"No," I said. "Scottish."

His eyes lit up. "That's an important distinction." Peter's features curved into a sly smile. For a man of ninety, he has finely tuned facial gestures. A holdover from a life in the stage, where each nod, wink, and bow can mean something important.

As I walked out of the kitchen with my tea, I stopped to admire a picture on the wall, hung over copper pots. It's from *Giselle*; Margot Fonteyn on the ground, the newly dead Giselle, and around her Rudolph Nureyev, as Albrecht, and Peter as Hilarion. Everywhere in Peter's house, even next to the pots and pans, were snapshots of ballet history.

Peter caught me considering the *Giselle* picture. "It's a dress rehearsal, although you'd never know it by Nureyev," he said. Nureyev was a brilliant performer, and even Peter will grant him that—but never as much so as when he was dancing with Margot Fonteyn. She tempered him. The magic was in the pairing.

Later, when I tried making tea at home, it didn't taste as good as Peter's. It required practice, a guiding hand.

When I think about Peter, I wonder if our backgrounds in dance paved the way for our unlikely friendship. Ballet for him lives in the stories he tells, and I recognize my own wish to live on in stories. I have a humble story, and yet when I listen to Peter, I hear humility there, too. So often, his stories of ballet aren't about him, they're about *her*. Margot Fonteyn.

They called each other "Daughter" and "Dad" as these were the characters they so often played on stage. "She dressed in Dior," Peter told me, pointing to pictures he has of her on tour. Margot may have been an international star, but for Peter, she lives in his stories as both a great friend and the hallmark of the classical tradition. Pulling out a gala program, he gestured to her upper body. "No one will ever have lines like that," he said.

So much of Peter's collected treasures are in homage to her. She is on his walls, in his library, always on his mind. He showed me a picture of the original cast of Sir Frederic Ashton's *Nocturne*, pointing out Margot before pointing out himself.

Part of Margot Fonteyn's international fame was sealed when she danced the role of Aurora in *The Sleeping Beauty* while on the American tour in the late 1950s. Ironically, Peter was often cast as Carabosse, the evil fairy whose spell is tempered by the benign counter spell of the Lilac Fairy, changing a death sentence into a hundred years of sleep. In real life, Peter would have never been party to such a fate. He's too alive.

Now, considering Margot and the role of Aurora, I think of my own ballet students and how so few would recognize the names of today's leading ballerinas. They often respond with blank expressions when I mention Dame Margot Fonteyn, prima ballerina assoluta. I find myself on Peter's quest, telling my own students, "If you're not familiar with her, check out YouTube," even though I know the black-and-white clips won't do her justice.

I have never danced Princess Aurora on stage, but I often feel I know her plight. I did not prick my finger and fall into a hundred years of sleep, but I did have a needle pricked into my arm, which revealed a disease that would still my body from the dancing it once knew. So, perhaps, a kind of sleep, dance kept dormant inside me. And if a prince's kiss didn't return me to dance, at least one major event—surgery— allowed me to reawaken to the art, if not as a dancer, then at least as a teacher. My story is not Fonteyn's, and I have no Peter to tell it after I am gone, but like him, I find myself yearning to make the past present, to tell those tales I have carried in sleeping muscles.

There are moments, too, in our unlikely pairing, when Peter and I don't talk ballet at all: Peter told me of his visits to the wound center after slipping on ice ("Such a bore," he complained); I tell him about my recent trip to Chicago, where I didn't make it out to any of that city's famous steak-houses ("Pity," he said. "But most are just overpriced."). Peter enjoys Formula One racing and thinks of driving, in his 1993 Honda, as a craft. I like to read poems. He likes to cook. Sometimes we just get caught up in being friends, even without the dance.

But ballet has its way of eventually inserting herself back into the conversation. For both of us, ballet is about what has passed, what we try desperately to preserve in words and pictures and other souvenirs. Though my house, downhill, isn't filled with pictures of great dancers, it does have its fair share of snapshots and old pointe shoes and programs. Relics of days gone by.

What is the drive to preserve? Is it the comfort of nostalgia, whose robust arms envelope us like a hug? I've not had a lot of formal training in history, but I have to think that our desire to study a history—personal, political, popular, or otherwise—stems from the need to better grasp who we are now. There is a backward-facing pull.

When I am with Peter, I often find myself letting go of who I once was, happy to take the trip with him through his memories. The need to tell becomes, instead, a desire to listen, an impetus a little like prayer. The more you listen, the more you are answered.

"That awful little man."

For as many pictures and books of Nureyev that Peter owns, this was the remark I'd come to expect when he talked of the great Tartar dancer. Tartar, not Russian, with the temperament to prove it. He would never properly rehearse. He would scream at the other dancers. He would scream at Margot, the greatest sin of all, according to my host.

Before we could talk of Nureyev, Peter assigned me "homework" in the form of one of Nureyev's biographies, one that Peter determined had "got it mostly right." For Peter, very few, if any, get it right, which, I suppose, is a dancer's mindset. We never get anything wholly right; there is always something to improve. So it is with dancing, and so it is with everything else.

I can tell you I heard a faint sneer in Peter's voice when he drew my attention to the dress rehearsal picture of *Giselle* above the copper pots in his kitchen. Only Peter and Margot are in dress, he noted, and there's *that awful little man* in his sweater tights, as if dressing for rehearsal was beneath him. I hardly witnessed joylessness from Peter except when he talked of Nureyev. For him, Nureyev represented reck-lessness—equal parts talent and carelessness—especially toward others.

"God only knows how many he infected," Peter said, referring to AIDS, the disease that would claim the uncon-querable Tartar. To say Nureyev slept around doesn't quite capture his sexual appetite. His exploits were nothing less than legendary, both according to the biography and to Peter.

Peter made it clear that what bothered him about Nureyev had nothing to do with his sexual orientation. In fact, Peter had spoken with warmth and affection of other dancers who were openly gay, recalling their days together in the company as anyone would speak of their old and dear friends. He often pointed out pictures of Alexander Grant, his easy smile betraying the friendship he missed. Grant, like Peter, was a principal dancer with the Royal, one who shared many of the same roles as Peter. He told a great story about how Grant and choreographer Frederick Ashton—Fred to Peter—had gotten lost in a borrowed car. It reminded me of antics from my own dancing days. Ballet companies have a reputation for being very stoic, full of discipline and work—and they can be—but there are days of hijinks, cutups, and fun. I remember when the entire Snow corps from *The Nutcracker* wore snowflake earrings instead of the requisite rhinestone studs, and how our choreographer simply hung his head in mock disappointment. It occurred to me, if only through my memory, that ballet breeds great friends, if, occasionally, a nemesis. It's just easier to focus on the nemesis.

Peter was less charitable to his former artistic director, Ninette de Valois, the woman responsible for bringing Rudi Nureyev into the Royal Ballet, and therefore into Peter's sphere. "She let him do whatever he wanted," he said, words spitting out as if his mouth were full of chalk.

The dislike of Nureyev had deep twin roots. Nureyev's cold and careless ways, and Peter's own deep admiration for Margot Fonteyn, whose legacy he protected with the determination of a knight errant. His chivalry included protecting her memory from all ugliness or stain, and so when talk turned to the inevitable question—did Margot and Rudi ever sleep together—Peter was resolute. "A person's private life is just that. Private."

For me, what has been private for so long are my struggles with rheumatoid arthritis. I have no famous couple to comment on, of course. Even if I did, I suppose that RA would still be that thing I'd want to keep private. It's not out of chivalry and friendship, like Peter's closed mouth. Mine is less selfless. I am not as graceful as Peter. I find it hard to expose this truth. But naming the thing that haunts you helps to rid it of its power, and perhaps Peter presented me with a guide to finding my voice. How do we know when to sing and when to be silent? I never asked. Perhaps I should have.

As to Fonteyn and Nureyev, no one has ever definitively confirmed what many have suspected about the onstage pair, whose palpable chemistry in front of an audience was part of their allure. I'd never asked about the affair, and if Peter tells me the truth, then I make him a promise that what he has told me will stay between him and me. Because, if nothing else, Peter and I have become friends, and above all, he considers me "a sensible girl."

At his birthday celebration, Peter made a toast to thank his boss—Queen Elizabeth II—making sure everyone had a drink or glass of wine. He celebrated his ninetieth year on earth surrounded by his Morgantown friends. I was the only guest there who had also been a dancer. It's hard to choose how to phrase that—meaning, I want to say that he and I "are" dancers, as though we are both actively engaged in the art of ballet. But that's not quite right, of course. And yet, it's perfectly correct.

We dined on a feast Peter cooked, a traditional English beef dish and chicken prepared in the Provençal style, which he learned, appropriately enough, while in France. The retired professor enjoyed the beef, while Peter's friend, the jeweler, asked about the wine. Peter complained about his doctor's appointments—"what a bore"—and how slowly his wound from the winter was healing. "Nothing heals as it should," he said. "Fast." In his company, Peter reminded me how much life he still had to live and how he wasn't letting age slow him much. It wasn't so much what he said, but the way he acted, the purposefulness in even the little things he did, like pouring tea or wine.

Dance has fashioned Peter into a true gentleman, made him thoughtful and easy to be around. He has met, learned from, and worked with extraordinarily interesting and creatively gifted people. He has morphed into one of them, and it draws other people to him. At his birthday celebration, this seemed very clear to me. I couldn't help but wonder if, perhaps, one day I might become a true lady, letting the extraordinary people, like Peter, like my past teachers and other dancers, influence my own character enough that I could become something better than myself. Get it right, perhaps.

We are all still in the long process of learning how to be.

And then there is dance, which for both Peter and me was as much a part of us as our height or eye color or skin. At its essence, I believe dancing is about joy. For us ordinary humans, joy is this huge, difficult, messy thing to handle. Dance tries to tame joy's messiness through technique and steps and the pursuit of defying gravity. But in the end, to really be a dancer, you have to soak in the joy, like a bath that leaves your hands prune-like. Dancers become, in their best moments on and off stage, vehicles for joy. And among his friends, this former Royal radiates that same kind of joy toward all in attendance.

As for me, it's like I'm a child stuffing my pockets full of candy, but instead it's this joy. It spills out and fades, but I keep lining those pockets in hopes it might stay.

Returning home after the festivities, a quick jaunt down a zigzag of streets, I considered where we lived. Our neighborhood was a quiet place filled with a collection of folks: university professors and pharmaceutical chemists and retired miners and Orkin men and fledgling writers. A place where lawns are mowed regularly and grandparents filled swimming pools in the summer so the grandkids would visit. Where people would walk dogs—beagles and boxers and labs and miniature pinschers and Boston bulls. Flying WVs decorate lawn flags and car decals. At the top of a hill in this neighborhood lived a man who was as Royal as the ballet company he danced for, a man who sometimes drank champagne in the afternoon, in his unassuming house, dreaming of past castles.

Certified: Dancer Becomes a Teacher

HERE'S A BIT OF ADVICE: if you're going to fly and you happened to have had a knee replacement, be ready for a pat-down at the airport after your artificial joint sets off the sensors. At airport security, I explain that I have rheumatoid arthritis. At first, the TSA agent acts suspicious of me, but after explaining my ailment and my reason for a total knee replacement, that seems to clear things up. "We'll be done in a minute, honey," she says. "Not so bad, is it?"

It is bad, but I don't blame her for doing her job.

The Pittsburgh airport seems like a poor place to enter into a debate on how disability is viewed and how the disabled are treated in this country. Homeland Security isn't in the business of being sensitive to feelings. Being led into a see-through holding area, then scanned with a wand and patted down does seem extreme for someone whose only offense was needing a premature joint replacement. Holding my tongue, I gather my belongings from bins, slip on my shoes, and proceed to my gate. I'm flying into La Guardia, then cabbing it to Chelsea, to Sacred Heart Residence. Tomorrow, I'll start the National Teaching Curriculum certification program at American Ballet Theatre.

Going to New York for this training is a minor miracle. After battling RA for nearly fifteen years, a part of me believed my studio days were finished. But with advances in my medication, and the knee replacement that sets off airport alarms, I'm able to renew my connection to ballet through teaching. I'm making a journey, not just to learn to be a better ballet teacher but to return to my past, to my first love: dancing.

In New York, I wonder if I stick out as an outsider, an interloper from Morgantown. I've been to New York before, but it feels fresh to me. When I was young, it didn't matter what strange city I was going to in order to study ballet. It all felt like a blank, open page where I could begin a new story. I would take classes all day, learn from new teachers. Sometimes perform. When I first left home, my sense of possibility grew with each pair of tights I packed in my suitcase. Maybe this is where I would flourish and grow. Maybe this is where I belonged. The location didn't matter—it could be Miami or Milwaukee, northern Michigan or New York. Back then, everything was ahead of me, and now New York is ahead, and it's like the blank page again. Sure, the context has changed, but there is that familiar pull of what can be, what I might become because of the training I'm about to receive.

What I know about New York, too, is the famous energy, the town, as Sinatra sang, that never sleeps. There is dance everywhere in New York, companies and schools and people busking in the subways and parks. I'm staying just a few blocks from the Joyce Theater, where the modern dance company Pilobolus runs a show during the ten days I'm there. There's an ad for Paul Taylor on a passing bus. Permeated with performance, New York pulses with dance, formal and informal, the hustle of people on the streets and the cadence of traffic, a kind of choreography. New York is the town of hopefuls, after all, the place where jars of change are saved for bus tickets and airfare.

After checking in at Sacred Heart, a boardinghouse run by nuns—yes, nuns—I hit the streets, looking for a branch of the public library so I can log in and check email. It's a welcome distraction. Nerves pinch and bundle. I've only recently started teaching ballet, and I am still figuring out how to teach. As a dancer, I might know something, but as a teacher I have to be able to articulate it, either in words or movement, or both. I'm struggling with how to translate what I know.

Fast forward to New York City and ABT's Training. I'd never really thought about teaching before I actually found myself in front of students. Now, I figure that if I'm going to teach, I need training so I can become a teacher like those who taught me—highly competent.

Because I do feel insecure explaining my long absence from dance, earning credentials from ABT feels like the kind of success that might give me greater confidence. Or maybe it is my own insecurity looking to be tamped down by accomplishment. I have always been this way, a seeker of accomplishments. It's not always a healthy thing, but it does keep me looking for ways to stretch and grow.

The choice is also intensely personal. To complete ABT training after all my health upheavals would be a personal triumph. The sense of anticipation feels just right, as if I could slip into my former self's tights, delicious with the sense of possibility, and not be resigned to a chronic disease.

In a way, it's not so much traveling out of town, but back in time.

I've found a way to end up in big midwestern cities—big small towns, as I've come to know them. Columbus, Ohio. Indianapolis, Indiana. Milwaukee, Wisconsin. There was something inviting about the dorms at the University of Wisconsin–Milwaukee, where I bunked during my summer intensive at Milwaukee Ballet. A basketball camp was located in another tower of rooms. We saw the boys around the campus, in the cafeteria, as well as when we caught our shuttle back and forth from Milwaukee Ballet's studios, where during the commute I often listened to Depeche Mode on my bright yellow Sony Sports Walkman. In the evenings, still light out and warm, I'd walk with my friend Maggie, a spunky girl who had a blond bob and not the long locks of most of the ballet students. We'd go to a nearby coffee shop, a funky little place that made the experience feel more like college than a ballet intensive. We mostly drank herbal tea, no caffeine, no sugar or fat. Still a teenager, I felt sophisticated sitting among college students and professors, watching people walk by with arms full of books, walking dogs, or couples holding hands.

During the days, I took class after class and loved it. I wasn't the best student at the intensive but not the worst either. I got a lot of attention, especially from a teacher with wavy, shoulder-length brown hair, and big spooky brown eyes that missed nothing. She wore T-shirts tied at the waist in a big knot, and had long, reedy legs. She demonstrated the combinations beautifully, but it was her constant eye on me that pushed me to get better. I swore she gave long, complicated adagios because she knew they were what I most needed to work on.

When I think back to summer programs, Milwaukee
stands out. Milwaukee is not New York, of course, but
the training I received there felt so organic. I know that I
improved, a feeling that gave me a new, quiet confidence.
I made friends and felt a part of the group. When dancing,
I didn't always feel included. There were always teacher
favorites, and often I was not one of them. I don't know that
I was a favorite at Milwaukee Ballet, but I received encouragement enough to feel like I merited attention. Even though
there was competition, and even though, like all my dance
training, it was tough, I felt that I was exactly where I was
supposed to be. I opened myself up to the work in a way
that also gave me a great sense of purpose. I let go of res-
ervations I had about myself and my abilities, and just gave
myself over to the experience of training. In the evenings,
physically tired, I let myself be a teenage girl in a strange
city, drinking hot tea with a friend, leafing through fashion
magazines. In the morning, fruit and coffee and nonfat
yogurt before starting the whole thing over again.

Chelsea's streets are busy when I head to the library. I can't
help but watch the other people. Men in stylish denim,
women in light, breezy skirts. New Yorkers have a practiced nonchalance I admire, even as it unnerves me—not the
same as pedestrians around Morgantown, mostly students,
sometimes profs, the occasional professional. New Yorkers
are purposeful walkers; from behind aviators and Wayfar-
ers, they march in time with the bustle of traffic and other
pedestrians. Only the dog owners keep a different, slower
tempo. I'm surprised by how many dogs I see walking the
streets of Chelsea: Golden Retrievers and Chihuahuas and
everything in between. Their paws click on the sidewalk
like the kitten heels of well-dressed women. Each breed has

a distinctive gait, unafraid to start or stop as they wish. In this way, I feel like it would be more fun to be one of the dogs of Chelsea. The dogs belong here in a way I don't, accustomed to the streets and routes of the neighborhood. I am aware of the buzz and clatter, but the dogs don't notice.

Sacred Heart's boardinghouse is, ironically, across the street from an Episcopal Seminary. An iron gate surrounds the seminary grounds, and large trees front massive brick buildings. All very secure. A man in shorts and sandals sits in an Adirondack chair on the grounds, reads under the shade of a tree. It's hot and unbearably muggy in New York, early August, and so there is something cool and lovely about sitting in my air-conditioned dorm room. A run-down camper rests parked in front of the seminary, the words *Omega* (the end) and *Chinook* (snow eater) printed on its side. It's a dingy cream color and tan-brown, its roof covered with debris. Garbage bags have been strewn across the hood, their black plastic held together with duct tape. The back tire is hopelessly flat.

I take a picture of it, because it seems both unlike New York and yet right in place, too. I tend to do that when I travel, finding my own off-kilter snapshots that speak to me at the time I'm visiting. Perhaps this is the luxury of new experience.

Isolation is a state that I only handle well when I want to be alone. Since arriving, I've felt isolated in a way that's very lonely, especially since I've not really talked with anyone. I have only "met" one of the sisters here at Sacred Heart. She speaks heavily accented English, using Spanish on the intercom. She wears a green T-shirt and pants, not a habit. So maybe she's not a nun. I haven't asked. When I arrived, I checked out the TV room on the ground floor. There's a big television, which is nice, but all the furniture is covered in clear plastic. There are also religious items about—crucifixes on walls, Baby Jesuses on end tables, Virgin Marys and Christs on the cross in random alcoves.

I am not Catholic, so the religious items strike me as strange, somewhat terrifying, but also beautiful in their own way. Perhaps this is the draw of religion, terrible and beautiful. Strangely, it also makes me feel safe, as if these items are imbued with protection. I'm not sure what I need to feel protected from, but I am looking for signs of safety. I suppose it doesn't make any sense since nothing is really threatening me. Still, everything is unfamiliar, different. And perhaps, paired with my own doubts about coming here for ABT training, that is enough.

In New York, you can pass amazing places and not even know it. The entrance to ABT's studios, 890 Broadway, next to an AMC Movie Theatre, is nondescript, but a line of bun-headed girls betrays the doorway and full elevators. The Young Dancer Summer Workshop is going on at the same time as teacher training. The elevator is packed with bodies going up, more queued and waiting almost as soon as I reach the fourth floor to register. This could have been me any number of summers, but of course I'm reminded of that summer in Milwaukee. I remember wearing a name tag for the placement class and feeling nervous and excited. When I look at these girls' faces, tight with anticipation and desire, often lightly freckled, I can't help but feel anxious for them. Under skirts and shorts, they wear the seamed tights I liked to wear when I was their age. Their hair pinned back with little rhinestone bobby pins or a chiffon flower, also something I would have done.

Once checked in, paying the last of my fees, I sit in Studio Nine, our classroom for the week. I watch other teacher training students filter in. Some sip coffee, others chat, but everyone checks each other out, the old sizing up habit from the performing days. The women, especially, stand turned out, many with the long bodies of their training, while I sit, feeling squat and out of shape. Small oval faces with delicate features, not unlike the students queued for the Young Dancer Summer Workshop, but with the signs of age, laugh lines and wrinkles. Perhaps even the wisdom of years performing. Feeling anxious again, I fold my hands together to keep from fidgeting. My black cropped pants and black T-shirt aren't so different from the others, and yet I'm acutely aware of the fact that I haven't danced in over a decade, while some in the growing group around me are clearly still in performance shape.

Studio Nine has a wall of windows, a wall of movable mirrors, and a wall of barres. Folding chairs have been placed for us to assemble classroom style. Some other students have taken seats, flipping through our course materials, a folder bearing a giant ABT logo and a two-inch binder with a collage of photos featuring ABT's Jacqueline Kennedy Onassis School students of various levels, genders, and ethnicities. All terribly official. Outside, New York blazes. Some students clump together in groups with people they know or recognize. I don't see any friends. It's as if I've been out too long, and now I've returned a mere tourist, a stranger.

Dancers, especially ballet dancers, have a look. There's a thin, whittled body, with long muscles that look as though they've been pulled like taffy. Despite the age range—mid-twenties to what looks like over sixty—we all have retained part of that pure balletic look. The dancers wait, some gingerly munching melon or other fruit provided by the training staff. Removed, I try to watch others without getting caught. Intimidation settles in my chest, so I doodle in my notebook, then concentrate just on breathing in and out.

You're here to learn, I remind myself. *You don't have to prove anything.* Just getting here, to ABT, a year after knee replacement, is a small accomplishment in itself. I've never been good at acknowledging accomplishments, though, especially small ones. And, because of RA, I don't look and feel like the dancer I once was, certainly not the girl who found her footing in the long-ago summer at Milwaukee Ballet. Sitting in Studio Nine, I feel, again, like the outsider, retreating into the newer me, the writer and observer. If I act like an observer, perhaps I can escape the growing awareness that, as a dancer, I'm way out of my league.

Nothing to prove, I remind myself.

Training begins when Raymond Lukens, a tall, middle-aged man with a dancer's carriage, calls our attention. He sits at the front on a tall barstool with a backrest, spreading a binder open across his lap. He gives lectures, and since I understand this approach, having so recently been in graduate school, I happily get lost in Raymond Lukens's initial talk on ABT's Ten Principles of Training and the Summary of Theory, forgetting to feel out of place for the moment. Then he gives us a rundown of what we can expect from our training. There are audible groans when he explains our exam—a two-hundred-point final with an oral and a written component. Exams. Now I feel definitely more at home. Not an audition, not judging my body and my technique, but assessing what I've learned and what I know. I may be the only person in the room without test anxiety. At least on the written part.

Raymond continues by explaining why the curriculum was created and offers a rundown of its goals. I find this interesting, because it is coming at ballet training from a different angle than the students. Pedagogy interests me because it helps clarify what I learned before as a student. It excites me to understand how to make a dancer, the kind who would be trained for ABT, adaptable to a range of styles, and working on choreography from classic Petipa through Balanchine, Tharp, and even modern works by Paul Taylor or Merce Cunningham.

Raymond coauthored the training with ABT's school's principal, Franco De Vita. As he sits in front of us, Raymond looks distinguished but with a bit of puckishness that shows itself in witty remarks and jokes. He obviously likes to inflect teaching with humor. He can speak fluent English, French, Italian, and Spanish, and he slips into another languages if a student also speaks that language. His explanations are pithy; when he talks about turnout, one of the Ten Principles of Training, he says, "Turnout is to ballet what a tomato is to tomato sauce. No turnout, no ballet." He shrugs dramatically to emphasize his point.

I enjoy myself as I listen, furiously scratch notes so I won't forget anything. Raymond peppers his discussion of pedagogy with examples. While explaining chassé, he reminds us how much Tudor and Ashton loved using that step in choreography. Around me, there are nods, people who've danced those works—*Nocturne* and *The Leaves Are Fading*, perhaps. At home, I have a bookshelf dedicated to DVDs of ballets, and I make a note to look for the use of chassé in the works of each.

Ballet teachers must train their eye to diagnose problems with technique as students execute the steps. One cannot prescribe a remedy for a problem that isn't diagnosed or, worse, misdiagnosed. I love the idea that a problem can be diagnosed and solved, so unlike RA, which can be diagnosed but only managed. Unlike ballet technique, there's no pedagogy to fix RA.

The summer I went to the intensive at Milwaukee Ballet, we got to perform at the Pabst Theater, known simply as "the Pabst." I tried not to think of the Blue Ribbon beer label, but of course I did. The first time I went in, I remember thinking the theater was so beautiful with its rows of polished wood and red velvet seats. I was in a piece with six couples dancing together, incorporating some simple pas de deux work. What I remember about dancing this lighthearted piece, choreographed by one of our teachers, was how much fun it was to be lifted into the air. It only occurs to me now, as I sit in training, that all the steps in that choreography were steps we learned in our pas de deux class. Nothing more, but because it was given to us again as choreography, all the dancers in the piece thought of it as something special. Having an audience and a venue probably heightened that feeling. Now I understand it as another way of teaching us how to execute that vocabulary.

I see some of the little ones scurry from one studio to another during a break, and I remember my favorite summer again, dancing all day as they do. Just as I did years before, these children will get to do a workshop performance at the end of their two weeks. They are much younger than I was when I went to Milwaukee Ballet. Nine, ten, eleven, a few twelve-year-olds. We will get to watch them as part of our training, since they're learning from the ABT JKO School's teachers in the levels we're learning in our classes. I love seeing them smile and laugh as they pass and then file into the studios, leaving the hallways quiet again.

Around me, teachers eagerly scribble on pads of paper or in notebooks, just as I do. So now I sort of blend in. Still, I don't identify as one of them. Many of the other students are former ABT dancers. Some rather famous, in ballet circles, like Ted Kivitt and Christine Spizzo. Kivitt was a longtime principal dancer with ABT and has been artistic director for other ballet companies, and Spizzo, a former soloist at ABT and teacher at North Carolina School for the Arts. I gulp down anxiety, tamp the urge to get up and run out, and continue to furiously take notes. Listening keeps me seated. But I know I'm also stargazing, and honestly, I kind of love the idea that I'm sitting next to people I used to watch on stage. Emotionally, I vacillate; outwardly, I press pen to paper.

As Raymond plows though material—there's so much to get through—my hand cramps. He spends a lot of time on foundational principles because it helps children to adapt to physical limitations. We're reminded that not everyone's body is perfectly suited to classical ballet technique. I think, yes! That's me. As I fluctuate from feeling excluded to feeling included, I draw little stars around notes, like "not all bodies are perfect." Although a lot of bodies around me look pretty perfect. Some students have moved from the hard, metal folding chairs to the floor, where they splay legs into haphazard straddle splits, folding bodies forward to write. Others sit so straight that I find myself trying to mimic their posture.

Just as I'm starting to feel uncomfortable again, Raymond reminds us of the most important aspect of what we're doing: "When ballet enhances people's lives, it's a very good thing." In a day already filled with competing emotions, this comment strikes the resonate chord. When I look up at Raymond, or over at my famous classmates, I can only wonder if they feel what I am feeling. It seems almost childish to hope they do, but I make that wish anyway.

During the lectures, I try to keep myself focused on the training, the valuable insights that Raymond shares. But much like watching a ballet on stage, I find that little details often stand out to me more than the big picture. For instance, the asides and references to history make Raymond's training lively and entertaining. But also, they let me learn a little about him, as a person and as a teacher. When talking about the head, he interjects a tidbit. "A three-quarter view of the head was considered more attractive to Renaissance artists," he says. He looks at us straight on—en face, in ballet terms—then turns and tilts the head in croisée devant. More attractive, indeed, a sly profile, something offered and something hidden, secret.

At one point, he discusses trying to communicate with students, and I really perk up. "I was teaching a bunch of fourteen-year-old students, so I read that dreadful book *Midnight* because they told me it was the best thing they'd ever read."

Several people correct him. "*Twilight*."

"Oh whatever," he says, and rolls his eyes.

I have students who are in love with those books, too.

Later, making fun of how difficult it can be to teach, he suggests we all read *Lord of the Flies*, because "Children can be terrifying," he says with a knowing laugh. "Little girls are evil."

He smiles so sweetly, it's as if the devil made him do it.

Next Raymond dubs the boys bulldozers and wipes

his brow as if he has been laboring. These asides make Raymond compelling. What I'm hoping is that some of his wittiness rubs off on my teaching—that I can find ways to be humorous, to make jokes when the teaching feels difficult. Also, to find ways, like he does, to connect with my students.

There's no way I'm going to read *Twilight*, though. The writer and reader in me draws the line.

For dinner the nuns lay out a spread of roasted chicken legs and beans and applesauce. Nothing special, but I'm so famished after such a long day that I scarf it down. If people think all dancers starve, they're mistaken.

The nuns run a tight, clean residence. Although each floor has communal bathrooms, they're rather private— each shower has its own stall and doors, and the toilets are also housed in stalls. Compartmentalized like confession booths. The bathrooms smell like lemon cleaner. As in other places within Sacred Heart, the nuns have left helpful notes on the wall: "DON'T LEAVE A FILTHY TOILET. FLUSH IT!"

Going down to the small cafeteria in the basement of Sacred Heart to eat dinner, I spy one of the nuns, dressed in a white habit and veil. I want to talk with her, but she moves so briskly down the hall that I only catch a glimpse.

The dining room is arranged in four-seat square tables, and I end up sitting with two lovely Japanese girls underneath a three-dimensional painting of the Last Supper. We literally eat beneath the disciples. I could be eating below Judas or John or Peter.

Feeling alone and not having really talked to anyone for most of the day, I strike up a conversation with one of my dinner companions. She is studying English, as it turns out.

Around us there are younger girls at dinner, clearly dancers, thin, with the tell-tale turned out duck walk. Longish hair, longish legs, small heads, delicate faces. I have radar for dancers.

When I come up from the basement cafeteria after dinner, a nun in a white habit sits at the desk in the main office. I want to go in and talk to her, but she is on the phone when I pass, speaking in urgently inflected Spanish. I see the young dancers dressed up, and I overhear their chaperone tell another resident that they are off to see *South Pacific*.

Tonight, for me, there's homework. Yes, homework. I have to create an exercise for class tomorrow. I remember what was said earlier today about the importance of ritual. In the Primary Level, the students are lined up single file in the hall and enter class to create a sense that the dance studio is a special space. For me, the studio was a magical place when I was a young dancer; this training advocates for specifically invoking the rituals of class. Studios, in reality, are pretty dingy places, and very blank, with only barres and mirrors adorning them. Maybe some fading posters or pictures. The ritual helps create a sense of purpose or maybe even magic. Raymond is particularly fond of ritual, his tone nostalgic as he proclaimed that "we tend to discard ritual." Ritual readies the mind for learning and makes the moment important.

Instead of deciding on an exercise, I find myself musing about my own rituals. Little rituals, and personal ones. I don't write on the first page of my notebook or journal—as of late, a little forty-eight-page memo book called Field Notes—because I like the idea that the notebook will someday need a title page, and in the meantime, a pristine page awaits that future title. I can't think of any journals I've titled, but the possibility of a title is allure enough to begin on page two. Perhaps I understand that I'm on page two or further into my own story. The past is full, but also blank—it cannot be written any other way.

There are other rituals; I have many grooming rituals, both morning and evening varieties, and a lingering sense that I should put myself together better. It could be vanity, but there is a distinct feeling of presentation in these rites— the patting of creams, the smoothing of blush, the strokes of mascara, the rubbing of lotion. A new ritual is treating my scar from knee surgery; using a vitamin E stick, I massage the scar's length. Over time, it has faded from the angry, deep pink to a fleshier, flat streak. I keep the ritual of treating it, convinced that it will continue to heal, that the vitamin E will keep the scar supple, easier to bend. Maybe it will, or maybe it won't, but it's a ritual, morning and night, all the same. It's not so different from how a dancer prepares for a performance. There's the particular makeup and hair for each ballet, but also the personal rituals of breaking in performance shoes, setting sentimental or lucky objects in the dressing room. I had a stuffed dog named Sharky that my great-grandmother made for me when I was a little girl. My favorite stuffed animal, Sharky has been backstage at every performance. I feel like I should have brought Sharky along on this trip to New York. I yearn for comfort and luck.

I wake up famished and end up eating two bowls of Frosted Flakes with two cups of coffee. So much for a dancer's diet. At breakfast the young dancers try to rouse themselves with good breakfasts, provisions their chaperone bought yesterday at Trader Joe's. They wear ABT shirts from the Young Dancer Workshop. I remember when I went away for the summer to study, how exciting it was to be in a new place with new teachers. Always scared, I pretended to be fearless. Perhaps not much has changed. I will buy a T-shirt from the ABT teacher training, just like I collected shirts before. I had a sweatshirt from Milwaukee Ballet that was bright red, the two Ls in "ballet" formed into a dancer's legs in first position. Another, from Pacific Northwest Ballet, showcases a ballerina leaping across the front. I miss collecting these mementos.

Today we're put into groups to share an original exercise from the Primary Level material we learned the day before. We'll get feedback from the ABT faculty. Interestingly, the ABT trainers keep telling us about using "imaginative imagery" to explain steps and concepts to students. The writer in me perks up. But that same writer feels let down by the imagery I hear—it doesn't strike me as particularly inventive. In fact, it's rather pedestrian. Hipbones forward like headlights, for example. I heard examples like this all the time coming up through the ranks. Maybe I bristle at it because I spent too much time in graduate writing workshops, where every word choice was analyzed. So it's strange to be in a place where I'm told words matter, but in actuality they end up mattering a lot less than what I might scrawl in my notebook to describe what's going on. Dancers are, even as teachers, still creatures of movement, and the verbalizing of dance is a landscape that remains quite unexplored. We communicate primarily with bodies. Yet I wonder if I've become more writer than dancer. It's strange how I can't wholly identify as a dancer anymore, but the same is true about becoming a writer, as though I'm stuck, a strange hybrid, the way fish and woman make mermaid.

Kate Lydon, a former ABT dancer and one of the teachers at JKO School, works with my group. The first time I've received direct and personal feedback, Kate tries to explain to me the difference between a gallop and a trot. "The trot is more of a prancing movement," she says. We trot a few steps together. A gallop is faster and syncopated. These are designed for five-year-olds, an age group I've never worked with, which shows in my exercise. I'm embarrassed, though—if I can't show the difference between trot and gallop, what will I do when we get into actual ballet technique?

No one in my group laughs or comments, and yet I feel humiliated. I don't want to fail. I try to think of it as one little bump, and refocus on other opportunities to come, but I can't help but question whether I should be here trying to earn this certification. Intellectually, I know these exercises are learning experiences—we aren't perfect and can get helpful feedback. But the pressure I've put on myself to be good at them causes my embarrassment to bubble up. I feel something akin to that desire to please my teacher in ballet class as a kid. I just wish to be good.

Training continues in long days full of information, sharing, watching classes, and then repeating the process. Luckily, Raymond Lukens continues to be entertaining. He tells us a story about his former school in Italy when he explains the importance of using the head and arms together in port de bras. In Italy, he had as clientele the wives of famous fashion designers. They were adult beginner students at his school. "Christmas in Italy was the best," he says of the lavish presents from Mrs. Feragamo and Mrs. Gucci. He had problems getting them to use their heads in class, however, because of the elaborate coiffed hairdos fashionable at the time he was teaching. "It was the eighties," he says. "Think of *Designing Women*."

Raymond gives us little breaks with helpful asides. He tells us he took jazz, acro, and even baton growing up, in addition to ballet. "Baton became really useful later on," he says. "As ballet master at Boston Ballet, I had to teach Sarah Lamb how to twirl the baton in *Stars and Stripes*."

I know these aren't the important aspects we'll be tested on, but Raymond's stories become my favorite parts of training. An aspect I have always liked about ballet is the stories. When my teachers would tell me stories, I soaked them in. Not all of them directly related to ballet, but that was perfectly fine with me. Stories, relevant or tangential, made me feel more connected to the lives of dancers. Some were so outlandish, and yet they are the stories I remember best. One of my teachers, Mr. Franklin, once told us a story about a dancer who couldn't find work in classical ballet so she went to Vegas to become a showgirl. He found out that she was doing *Swan Lake* at one of the casinos: "Imagine my surprise seeing Dying Swan topless." The class, a collection of teenaged students, stood with mouths agape. Mr. F., as we called him, would contort his face in mock horror before adding, "So girls, if you can't get a job, go to college, not Vegas."

Even as the days continue, I'm not overly social with other students until I find an empty seat next to a stylish woman with short reddish-brown hair with a funky blond streak. She has a welcoming smile and introduces herself as Laurie Picinich-Byrd, artistic director of the Florida Ballet in Jacksonville. She and her late husband founded the company and now she runs the company and school herself. She's a tiny woman, a little firecracker, who makes funny asides during class. I like her; we eat lunch together. Everyone I meet, including Laurie, asks me about West Virginia when

I tell them I live in Morgantown, curious about the mountains and about my classes at the university.

"So you teach ballet and writing?" Laurie asks, and then munches on her salad.

"I teach in the Multidisciplinary Studies program," I say before taking a bite of egg salad sandwich.

She nods. "Interesting," she says and smiles. "That sounds like fun." It had never occurred to me that anyone in my training would think my combination of writing and ballet would be interesting.

When I tell her I have rheumatoid arthritis, she asks if it bothers me, and for the first time I'm aware that while I've been in New York I've not had any flares. "I'm managing," I tell her and it's true.

Laurie tells me a little about her company and school. "You know, the economy forced me to cut back on the company," she explains. The Florida Ballet Company's board helped finance her ABT training to build their school. Laurie is older than me, but I can't really get a fix on her age, nor do I want to be impolite and ask her. But it is clear by the way she talks that she has trained many dancers.

"We had a couple kids make the finals of Grand Prix," she says. The Youth America Grand Prix is a ballet competition for serious students. She forks lettuce with her plastic ware.

When Laurie talks about her students, there's pride in her voice, as if they were her own children. Not boasting, but the kind of pride that shows when a teacher commits to helping her students, and the students accomplish things. She has sent students on to selective college programs and to companies, which I find impressive.

"You know, I'm getting really nervous about the exam," she says. I'm surprised by her confession, her voice unsure for the first time since I've met her.

"I make these flash cards," I say, showing her a deck of three-by-five cards wrapped in a large rubber band. "It helps with the nerves."

"That's a great idea," she says, considering the stack. "There's a lot to memorize."

"We can meet after class or on break and go over them," I say, collecting up the remnants from lunch to throw in the garbage. She agrees, and I have made my first study buddy. I no longer feel so totally on the outside looking in but am someone with something to offer.

After lunch, we break into groups to show exercises again, this time for a different level. Laurie is in my group and we sit together. My exercise, a simple sauté combination, goes over much better than past ones, and I feel more confident. I picked it because as a student I loved jumping, and so to get my confidence up, I chose something I liked. But now I also have a legitimate friend who gives me an approving smile and nod after I present my work. Christine Spizzo, the former ABT soloist, is also in our group, and Laurie and I whisper that we love watching her demonstrate her exercise. Although retired from performing, Christine is still lithe and her legs are perfectly turned out.

During the break after our exercise presentations, Christine comes over to talk with Laurie and me.

"I was so nervous," she says, lightly touching Laurie's arm. Although I don't say it, I'm shocked, because she certainly didn't look nervous. Christine has chatted with the majority of students in the training and has made friends with nearly everyone. If there were a Miss Congeniality award given to a student in the training session, it would be her for sure.

"I wrote your combination down," I say, and point to it in my little Field Notes book. During the next review session, I notice more and more people taking notes.

The summer in Milwaukee, I made friends quickly, something I didn't always do at other intensives. Because of the competitive nature of the programs, friendships didn't always grow. I wonder now if I've brought that old mentality with me to the ABT training, that as a way of protecting myself I didn't invite more opportunity to make friends. I lost touch with Maggie, my pal at the Milwaukee Ballet Summer Intensive. Time and change do that, of course. Now it reminds me of how different I've become since then. Back then, my performing career was ahead of me. Maggie wouldn't even recognize me now. Sometimes, I don't recognize myself. But being at ABT has made me aware of how much, how deep down, I miss ballet, miss that young dancer in love with the idea of dancing at the Pabst. And so, as I make friends in the last days of ABT, I only hope I'll do better to keep in touch with these others who share my love of ballet and who are also now teachers. I already know that if I pass the Primary Level 3 exam that I will want to come back for the Level 4 and 5 training, and maybe even 6, 7, and Partnering, to complete it. I would love to come back with my new friends. But I don't want to assume I'll even pass the first levels.

There is, of course, the exam to take.

As a break from my ballet-centric days, I continue to get to know the Japanese girl at the boardinghouse at dinners. Her name is Tae, and she will start a graduate program at NYU soon. She says she likes talking with me because I speak clearly. She practices English by having conversations with native speakers. I like having the company and focusing on things other than ballet.

Also at dinner, a woman named Blanca introduces herself and tells me she recognizes me from the training. She is older than me but with a young, open face. She's here from

Puerto Rico and is taking the training because her daughter, also a dancer and dance teacher, took it. Blanca tells me she was initially skeptical, but that she loves the training. I tell her I love it too, and it's the truth. Blanca and I start to study together. I continue to make flash cards; it has always been a good way for me to study. Blanca finds them helpful as well. We meet in the common areas and study, go back over all we have learned. Again, I find myself being accepted, making friends, and not feeling quite so intimidated or alone. I haven't gained comfort, but I have found camaraderie. It's a shame that it has come so close to the end of my stay in New York.

Before bed, I make more flash cards, review my notes, and then read a book that has nothing to do with dance to clear my head. Before I set my alarm, I set out my clothes for the next day and snap off my light, as I do each night. Rituals. I think Raymond is right about their comfort.

During this trip, I didn't stop to really think about why I decided to do American Ballet Theatre's National Training Curriculum certification. I know that it has something to do with my knee replacement surgery and a desire to overcome both the surgery and my ongoing struggles with rheumatoid arthritis. I don't like the idea of RA limiting me. Some people who know me might think I'm trying to prove my ability to other people, but I truly believe that the real skeptic, the person I feel I have to prove something to, is me. Sure, I wanted to gain knowledge and be the best ballet teacher I could be. But the deep-down reason I went to ABT is to show that I can still have a place in the world of ballet. It's about being viable. About not accepting defeat. Selfish though those things may be, they are all part of it, part of my complicated relationship to the disease and how I live my life with it, keeping my enduring devotion to the art of ballet. Even when I wasn't dancing, the idea of dance lingered in me still. First loves are like that.

The night before the exam brings fitful sleep, but I arrive at the Broadway studios well ahead of time, have a coffee, and start with the written exam.

The written exam is the part I have the best shot of doing well on. I'm a decent test taker when I'm prepared, and I've been working the flash cards all week, so it does feel like I know the material. Not that I let myself be overconfident. I check the answers three times before turning them in.

My oral exam is a different story. Because I have been so far removed from my own dancing experience, compounded with the toll rheumatoid arthritis has taken on my body over the years, and just the fear of being examined in this format, I am terrified. I try to keep calm by not focusing on any of those things. We have been divided into groups and given a time slot. Each of us will present to an instructor: Raymond, Harriet, Kate, or Franco, with a second person in the room as a proctor. The examiner and proctor will make detailed notes, and we will be scored. My examiner will be Franco De Vita. I don't know him and only saw him teach once. I tell myself the only thing I can to calm myself: if I pass this test, I can be sure that I really know the material because I was tested by the ABT School's principal himself.

The exams take place in various offices, and halls serve as waiting areas for us, tense columns of space. We watch our peers emerge slack-faced and white from the examination rooms. I know why we must be tested: before one of the world's most respected ballet organizations can give us their stamp of approval, there has to be some mechanism to show that we've earned that approval, that we are, in fact, their *certified* teachers. It sets ABT's training apart from many others I considered. What made me choose ABT now scares me.

When I enter the exam room to face Franco, I will myself not to shake. As we work through the questions, I try to be thoughtful, respectful. I answer the best I can, and have to ask him once to clarify because I don't quite understand his English. He gently corrects my arm once.

"Not wrong," he says as he gently shapes my arm. "Making more right." He notices my swollen knuckles, and I tell him about my RA, and he says something that is very hopeful. "Is okay. I have not so good grand plié, so I don't demonstrate full out. Give the students the sense of the movement."

I find this advice both consoling and devastating. Is he trying to say I've passed and here's my advice, or be nice about the fact that there's no way I'll be an ABT certified teacher? I won't know for over a month, when the exams are scored and sent to us in the mail. A small eternity.

When I leave ABT's studios, I put on my sunglasses, not just to block the sun, but so I can cry without it being noticed. When I get back to my room, I let myself weep for about fifteen minutes before doing anything else. The training has been an emotional and mental marathon, so much in such a short time that I need a release. After a good cry, I pull it together, willing the tears dry. Then I go wash my face with cold water, and pack my things, including my giant binder, not just full of notes, but cards and slips of paper with the contact information of my new friends.

Even before I leave, I know I will miss New York, with fond longing for my short time at ABT. A small part of me belongs to this time and place, which was tough and scary and, above all, quietly magical. I want to keep it perfect in my memory, but like all things ballet, it's a snow globe of swirling particles, tiny bits of memory shaken up as a reminder of what once happened.

The last thing I see is not ABT's studios but the broken-down camper across from Sacred Heart. It has not changed since I arrived and may not change at all for some time. It's just as hot, humid. The cab fare to La Guardia is outrageous, but no more so than when I came into the city. The airport is cool, and my bag is just under the weight limit as I check in and prepare for the security pat-down again. I'm too tired to be upset about the TSA. The airplane trip is nondescript; I halfheartedly read a book as we head for Pittsburgh. Then it will only be an hour-and-a-half drive and I will be home in West Virginia, my travels having come full circle. And yet, I know I have changed, have done something both new and familiar. I went away and returned, as Raymond said, with my life enhanced, which is a very good thing. What I proved, more than anything else, is that returning to ballet in any form is to honor who and what I am. And while I'll never be a famous dancer, I have new tools to share this tremendous, beautiful, terrifying art. My faith in myself may have waned, but I didn't give up.

Now, I wait for the results.

One year and nearly three months after I've had knee replacement surgery, and about one month after returning from the training, I receive an official-looking manila envelope in the mail from the National Training Curriculum program at American Ballet Theatre, with the silver, white, and golden ABT logo. I open it, hands trembling. The paper is thick and crisp in my hands.

Claque

IMAGINE THE THEATER, the proscenium stage, the layers of balconies like tiers of wedding cake. The audiences peppered with claqueurs, those professional appreciators of spectacle. What in us yearns for their applause? Perhaps my teenaged self knew better than I do now. I know that recognition still feels important, but the need has changed forms. Still the promise of applause, hands striking together in a vigorous rush of sound, rolls over the performers and envelops them. Such pleasure gained from simple sound is a feeling one doesn't forget.

The word *claque* makes me think of two things. The first is a variation from act 2 of the ballet *Raymonda*. The other is old Paris, as if I knew it beyond the books I've read and pictures I've seen. Conjured up in my imagination, it has a bluish, Degas-inspired wash of color, the tattered tulle of romantic-length tutu, dancers' young ecstatic faces upturned into light. Certainly those performances have claqueurs, spectators who applaud for hire. Who would be the chef de claqueurs, organizing a series of well-placed cues, like the laugh tracks used in sitcoms? It's all done to demonstrate approval. Yet as I think about approval, I end up musing on friendship.

Although I've always had friends, I can see that there have been times in my life when I've struggled making them. I've wanted approval from friends, whether to like me or to appreciate my work. It seems a lot to ask of another human being and a lot to give another. The times when the challenge of making friends felt most acute tend to coincide with my own moments of applause, times when I received some measure of appreciation while making art. It happened first through dancing and later through writing. Perhaps art requires a kind of selfishness, an inward looking to make an outward product. I am skeptical, though. Still, approval shifts from the personal, one-to-one interaction to the result, an audience's gaze. Maybe I've just never been good at managing the difference.

However, the older I get, the less the memories are of performance or approval. As the clamor of the claques fade, the smell of studio sweat and the tunes from upright pianos and variable-speed record players fill my senses. Pinched-front leotards, slippers with thick elastics, holes worn through the soles. The studio is what I remember most. The studio, not the stage, is what made me a dancer.

Raymonda usually wore a white, champagne, or light blue tutu, but in variations class I added only a blue chiffon shirt to my pink tights and my navy camisole leotard. My mother made skirts with lovingly serged edges and grosgrain ribbon waists. It was the late 1980s, it was Florida, hot and humid, even with air conditioning blasting. I soaked in sweat all the time. My teacher, Mrs. Gooden, decided to teach us the Claque variation from *Raymonda* in our pointe class.

Mrs. Gooden's feet were the stretchiest, most perfect ballet feet I ever saw. When she wasn't dancing, she wore high-heeled sandals that made her legs look long and lean. Mrs. Gooden was trim without looking brittle, the way some other ballet teachers looked as they aged. Others filled out into post-dancing bodies. Mrs. Gooden demonstrated in class, with her impossibly beautiful feet. I remember something else: for lunch she ate half a peanut butter and jelly sandwich, cut-up veggies, and two Keebler chocolate chip cookies.

I adored her.

Mrs. Gooden didn't teach at a fancy training center or company school. Her studio was housed within a selective private school in Fort Lauderdale, Florida, known for academics. Dancers found her, though. Some drove from as far away as Miami and West Palm Beach, braving I-95's notorious traffic, to take her open classes. I was one of those dancers.

Desirée and I met at a summer intensive at Interlochen Center for the Arts in Michigan, and she became my best friend in Mrs. Gooden's class in Ft. Lauderdale. It's not so strange for dancers to keep meeting up with one another in different parts of the country. Desirée had much nicer port de bras than I did. I could jump higher, farther, and faster. We joked that together that we made a complete dancer. We always danced together, unless the teacher separated us, which rarely happened because we didn't talk or disrupt class.

As I remember it, Desirée's favorite variation was the Claque. I could never pick a favorite because I wanted to dance them all. Kitri's fan variation, anything from *The*

Sleeping Beauty, Gamzatti's wedding variation from *La Bayadère*. I could never get enough. *Raymonda* wasn't much of a ballet. With a thin plot, it was a nineteenth-century relic designed to show off a growing corps of dancers. It's not danced often, but it's still around, and I think that's due to the rich score by Glazunov.

The Claque variation features music that sounded haughty and moody, and my teenaged self believed this represented Russian princesses as they once were. The variation forces a dancer to inhabit a certain kind of character, one self-confident and assured, regal, perhaps more than what a teenager can reasonably achieve. With age comes nuance. The variation began with simple movements. Deceptively simple: mostly poses and bourrées, which could look awful if the dancer didn't commit to perfection. Simplicity remained a tricky ideal. For this reason, the Claque wasn't a good variation for dancers who only excelled technically. The simplicity required stage presence, imbuing every little gesture with a sense of confidence. This is why simple movement is difficult; in solo dancing, simple movement is paramount. It is an artistic, not just a technical, test, where the dancer owns the movement and makes it her own.

Variations, called such because there are often versions of solo dances changed to suit an individual dancer's needs, were fun to learn because they reminded us students that the goal of learning technique was to perform. This intermediate step often had no audience, but the pieces we learned were from the stage. Our teachers had learned them and passed them to us. And while there are many good books on ballet technique, you can't learn ballet from a book. It's passed from dancer to dancer.

I've read the stories of the ballets, and something about *Raymonda* that sticks out is not from act 3, where the Claque is pulled, but from act 1. Raymonda goes to the enchanted garden of dreams where she dreams of her beloved. When I am writing, it's like entering that enchanted garden, but the dreams are really memories that play out in my imagination, as if my old self were a character invented for ballet. They are both me and completely distant from me. While I've become something different from the dancer I once was, I go to the page looking for my beloved, dancing itself. In this garden, a vine of ivy might lead to those days in Mrs. Gooden's studio, my good teacher, my unlikely friend.

Maybe these moments were never the way we remember them, just like a ballet never quite looks or feels like real life. Mrs. Gooden, as wonderful a teacher as she was, could never be my fairy godmother; nor could Desirée be the plucky friend of so many of ballet's heroines. We are too nuanced in feeling and not nuanced enough in physical gesture for this to be so. Perhaps this why my memories have strayed from performance, relocating to the studio. That is where we lived and breathed and worked. The studio helped us conjure dreams but was never a dreamscape.

What I'm saying is that no one would break out in applause because Desirée and I found our friendship in the unlikely setting of the dance studio. Despite this lack of outward recognition, our friendship was more remarkable than the feats onstage.

Things I remember: I liked tights with seams down the back and Desirée did not. My hair was darker and Desirée's was more honey-toned. We were not required to wear a specific leotard or color for class. As soon as we heard the needle hit the record, we stopped any chatter and committed ourselves to the regimen of ballet. In her studio, Mrs. Gooden had an old turntable with a knob that allowed her to speed up or slow down the music, so she could adjust it to the tempo she wanted. And tempos often changed. But what I really remember was the music itself. Mrs. Gooden played a lot of standards, and when I think of her class, I can always hear the strains of "Penny Lane" from a well-known record of ballet class music by a pianist named Lynn Stanford. Most likely, dancers who came up through the ranks of ballet in the 1980s knew these records well. "Penny Lane" transformed into grands battements. I can't even hear the Beatles' version without wanting to toss my leg high into the air.

Many decades removed from learning the Claque variation, I found myself not only writing about dance but also teaching ballet. I have, in fact, taught the same variation from *Raymonda* that Mrs. Gooden taught to us those many years ago. Teaching ballet isn't exactly what I thought I'd be doing in my thirties and forties, but I can't say I regret that it's happened. In teaching, I've learned to be patient, empathetic, and perhaps giving in a way that I'd not been before. In teaching, I've gained a kind of openness that reveals less selfishness. Perhaps the teacher in me has gained from learning the ways of friendship, from dancers like Desirée, my long-ago studio pal, and Mrs. Gooden, the teacher I most emulate. It could be that the two cannot be split. Friendship instructs us in the techniques of empathy.

I've taught in private studios, preprofessional training centers, and in university settings. Despite the differences, the one thing that I try to do in each is to emulate Mrs. Gooden. Her love for young dancers was nested in every correction she gave us. *Resist the opposite shoulder back. Coil and turn. Push down to stay up.* I use her active verbs, trying to get just the right effect—*stretch* when the jerky look of *straighten* won't do. Like her, I try to teach to every student in the class; everyone requires attention and deserves good training, whether they are there for the joy of movement or for training for a professional career. Each body deserves to move in the right way, with grace, with the ability to remain injury-free. Mrs. Gooden gave her lessons equally to all of us and with a lightness of being I can only categorize as joy. I cannot remember a time when I saw her frown.

When one of my students was accepted to a competitive sum-mer intensive program through an audition process, I was proud of her. Meghan has the long body of a Balanchine dancer and feet effortlessly pliant. Her skin is smooth and olive, and when she smiles in class, it's always slightly crooked, like she's holding a secret under her tongue. Naturally flexible, her legs unfurl into developpé in the slow tempo of a dollop of syrup.

At first, Meghan was unsure if she would go to the summer intensive. Then she had a change of heart. "At first I couldn't believe I was the one selected," she told me one day after class. "And then I thought about all the people I would meet."

Now, she seems excited at the prospect of going away, her large brown eyes twinkling when she wonders out loud who her roommate this summer might be. I think to myself, yes, Meghan. That's it—that's exactly how to go away this summer. Learn everything you can, and learn especially how to be with others. This experience is more than dancing.

Desirée was the one friend I had within the world of the studio who was not a rival. She wanted to go to college to study art history. Intelligent, she kept her grades high enough that she could go to nearly any college she chose. While I earned good grades, all I wanted to do was dance in a ballet company. I rarely gave a thought to anything else. I yearned for dancing. Our different futures didn't keep us from friendship, though, or from working hard in class together.

There was a part of me that envied her interest in academics. Dancer in training first, I still aimed for high grades and was a good student. When Desirée talked about potential colleges—Vassar, Columbia, Swarthmore—they sounded exotic and upper-crust and something, perhaps, beyond what I could do. I imagined gray sweatshirts emblazoned with crests or large block letters. Libraries with antique lamps, endless shelves of books. I suppose I imagined it like a set for a play about college, trying to put myself for just a moment into the world Desirée chose for herself. Maybe it was an attempt to support her choice.

When I think about friendship, I think about this time in my life, this dancing beyond applause. I accepted Desirée as my friend, perhaps because Desirée danced without the ambition of a professional career. But I hope we'd be friends even if she did choose to dance. I again wonder about the ability of applause to hamper friendship—that desperate need for approval and appreciation. Where does that leave friendship? Though I had this early model of what it meant to have a friend, I didn't really learn to be a friend until much later. It took decades to understand that art and friendship need not live in separate spaces. The heart, once conditioned, has strength enough for both.

I can never adequately express what it means that Desirée liked me beyond the dance studio. She was one of the first people outside my family with whom I freely laughed and cried. I never felt I could confide in other dancers. I was in competition with them. It made friendships difficult.

With Desirée, friendship came easy. Not only could we talk about things outside the studio, she could also understand how difficult ballet training was and how frustrating it often became to me. A couple times I felt like quitting, but Desirée was always saying funny things, like "You can't quit, you have to go to a company for both of us." Or, "You'll end up wanting to get an art history degree like me," and making a face like in Edvard Munch's "The Scream." With her big, doe-like brown eyes, smooth and pale skin, and honey-brunette hair, even posed as "The Scream," Desirée looked pretty.

My imagination often filled in the bits and sections of ballets I had learned to dance, and Raymonda, as I imaged her, was just my kind of Russian princess: a bit arrogant and sassy but mostly blue-blooded and refined. When Mrs. Gooden demonstrated the quick-moving bourrées in the Claque variation, it looked as if her feet didn't touch the floor. Her long brown hair coiled into a bun that could rival even Martha Graham's huge, iconic knot. Little curls sprang next to her face between her temple and her ear. Other than these curls, her hair was impeccably neat. I loved the curls. They gave her face a kinder, less severe quality than other teachers.

In variations class, our efforts weren't performance-grade and weren't expected to be. Learning from the classical repertoire helped us understand how our daily technique would one day translate to the stage. It also helped us to know and learn those ballets, which we were encouraged to see performed.

Ballet insists on translation of meaning—story and character—into the technique, the steps themselves. Before I met and worked with Mrs. Gooden, my translation tended toward a shoddy interpretation—merely trying to keep up technically. As she improved my technical abilities, Mrs. Gooden taught me to speak ballet's language by becoming a character. Raymonda, in the Claque variation, became only one lesson in interpretation of many.

Some teachers rely on imitation to teach. These teachers show a combination and expect the pupils to get it, to absorb what they see and replicate it with their own bodies. Gifted students can do this; to some extent, my friend Desirée was able. And yet teachers other than Mrs. Gooden tended to overlook her because she had more curves than what they deemed acceptable. But Mrs. Gooden didn't pick favorites and she didn't discriminate based on body type.

I suppose my own reasons for choosing to work with Mrs. Gooden didn't differ much from my friend's. Perhaps my body had better ballet proportions, but I didn't absorb simply by watching, so some teachers twisted and wrenched me into the shape they wanted. Sadly, this rarely took either, which frustrated both me and the teachers. Because I didn't learn from being put into the right position or from imitation, I needed to have ballet explained to me; I needed to learn through language cues that made sense in my brain and could be translated into my limbs. I required words, images. Mrs. Gooden turned ballet into active verbs: release, stretch, coil, lengthen, snap, dart, and, of course, breathe. Static French terms no more, technique became dynamic and movement-based. Even poses required an active energy, balancing no longer a guess but a state of being. Energy flowed in all directions.

Luckily, I possessed some strengths as a dancer. Besides good feet—although never as amazing as Mrs. Gooden's—I had a strong sense of music. A waltz is different from a bright march. Different tempos or styles changed the articulation of the foot, the same way that two different routes can end up taking you to the same place. Mrs. Gooden created combinations that showed us every route.

Desirée's approach to dancing was visual, and her awareness was through the look of ballet. She sculpted her body, creating a visual that captured an emotion, feeling. I would bet that, even now, people can see her dance training in everyday movements, how she stands or sits or walks. I'll bet she's retained the graceful, elongated neck and open chest of the dancer she once was.

North to New York, west to Columbus and beyond, south through the Carolinas and Alabama and Florida, I go to see my dancers perform in their summer intensives. I travel because I am proud of their accomplishments, because they deserve an audience. And I go as homage to my own past, when I, too, went away and danced the end-of-term showcases.

It takes a certain kind of faith to go to a strange city at age eleven or twelve and to keep going through the teen years. Though helpful, a summer intensive is no guarantee for a future career. My father once explained the concept of faith to me as belief without proof, which I somehow remembered off-kilter as belief beyond proof. It makes the phrase "blind faith" redundant. All faith is blind, believing in what the heart can see rather than the eyes. To be a dancer takes faith. The outward signs will mostly point to failure. At a summer intensive, a young dancer sees hundreds just like her—good dancers with good training, all of whom might have a career—or might not have one. She goes with the faith she might, with hard work, become a professional.

I think about how I went to these programs, how now my students are going, and I wonder at my nearly masochistic desire to locate myself in the impossible spheres of art. Artistic disciplines can often be unforgiving. Rejection is high, real accomplishment low. To believe in a life of art is a faith approximating madness.

To make it in either ballet or writing should have been a triumph of my faith. If I never pursued an artistic discipline after dancing, to have reached a professional level would have been extraordinary; the hours put in, the desire that pushed me to never give up, the time I took away from being a "normal" kid, playing sports, joining clubs, and all that. To later decide that I would devote myself to writing, despite the years that could be spent crafting a work to only be told no over and over. To take it apart and assemble it again, and to know that people around me, even ones who cared deeply, thought it nearly crazy that I continue to try to make something beautiful from the choreography of words on a page, is overwhelming to think about. Maybe I can't think about it. It seems art is best when I'm doing it, actively engaged. To create a life in both stakes a claim to the impossible, and I can only suspect that it's my stubbornness, an overactive will, that eradicates any notion of giving up when the faith starts to wane. But I want it all, and with the love and support that only true friendships provide. It's a tall order, but shouldn't we want a life filled with largesse?

So I twine my art together, and I look for solace, and often find it first in teaching ballet. My students file into the studio, and as I feel the words of my teachers—especially Mrs. Gooden—escape my lips, I know that I am giving them good instruction. I return home to write, filled with how their bodies transform over the hours. Kira balanced forever; Maddie executed double pirouette and surprised herself. On paper, my students' daily, tiny victories are preserved in poems and stories and essays. Also, my young dancer self is resurrected, no longer *la belle au bois dormant*, awake even without a prince. When I reflect on it all, I cannot help but wonder, what would Desirée and Mrs. Gooden think about this life I've created? Would it meet their approval? I suppose I have faith that it might.

Desirée hardly ever missed class and neither did I. Sometimes on Fridays we'd sleep over at each other's houses. Mostly we talked about ballet, but sometimes music and boys. We listened to Echo and the Bunnymen, Depeche Mode, and The Cure on a CD player in Desirée's bedroom. Sometimes we acted like teenaged girls, but other times we were ballet obsessed, glossy *Dance* magazines strewn over freshly vacuumed carpet. I never asked her, but I wondered if the reason Desirée decided not to continue in ballet was because she didn't have the ideal ballet body. That made me sad, and still does, because she was so beautiful to watch. Desirée had effortless movement, a quality that was enviable to any other dancer.

During our sleepovers we would watch videos of ballets we loved, like *Don Quixote* and *The Sleeping Beauty*, falling asleep as they played.

Once, Desirée confided in me that she'd considered quitting ballet. In Mrs. Gooden's studio, she was happy dancing again. I never knew that she was unhappy dancing. Her unhappiness only revealed itself in bits and snippets of conversation over time.

Over the years, I have thought about this and wished I'd known better how to help my friend. Because when dancing, Desirée radiated. She was effortless without being careless, refined without being stiff. I wish I knew how to tell her just how lovely her dancing was without feeling like I'd betrayed myself. I wish I could have been the friend to her that she'd been to me.

While teaching us the Claque variation, Mrs. Gooden made sure we knew the basic story of *Raymonda*. She made sure we knew the score was by Glazunov and the choreography by Petipa. For her, this was all part of our training. We watched a video of the variation danced by Natalia Makarova, every gesture drenched in majesty. Although Makarova was tiny, she danced as if she took up the entire stage. She owned it. Her white tutu, embellished with champagne-colored lace and rhinestones, caught the stage lights, perceptible even on the VHS recording. Her legs and arms were impossibly slender.

Mrs. Gooden never simply taught us the steps to a variation. We learned everything about it. When we watched Makarova, she told us to watch how Makarova's arms told the story. They did. She embodied what I thought a Russian princess would look like as she got married. She placed them, as if arranging herself to be seen to advantage. Deliberate. Self-possessed. Everything I was not as a teenager taking ballet lessons. The whole class watched, hooked, hanging onto her every gesture.

Desirée imitated Makarova's gestures best. Though her arms were more muscular and substantial than Makarova's, she copied her bearing, giving her Claque variation polish. I'd say I envied the effect, but that's not quite the truth. I think I wanted to be able to translate gesture like Desirée did, but I was also proud of what my friend accomplished in learning the variation. We didn't have to be equally good at the same things. I had a few things that came more naturally to me, even in the Claque variation. For instance, the ending of the Claque: fast passés en relevé and sissonne pas de bourrée, movement that sped up with the music. Whip-fast pirouettes and chaînés.

What I remember best is correction. "Slice the back leg behind to really move the bourrées."

Slice—active verb.

To my knowledge, neither Desirée nor I performed the Claque on stage. Still, it is one of my favorite variations. I get chills when I see another perform it well, hearing the sound of her hands clapping together and then watching them separate, one on her hip, the other behind her head. Claque is from the French *claqueur*, meaning to clap and, of course, is the name given to that group of people hired to clap at a performance. Every Raymonda I've seen has deserved applause, even without the hired hands.

Over the years I've lost touch with Desirée. Like many friendships, we didn't survive time and distance, even though I think of her fondly, and I keep a picture of us, fresh-faced teenagers backstage at the ballet, on the bulletin board above my desk in my home office. Often, when I'm writing about dance, I'll look up, see our made-up, pre-performance faces. Our smiles are wide and genuine, full of excitement, reminding me of the joy of being a young dancer. Almost enough to make me clap for us, one more time, like we clapped at the end of each class, after the reverence, when we curtsied not to an audience but to the most important person, our teacher.

Fierce and Delicate

THE GIRLS FILE IN AND FACE THE BARRE. We begin with a warm-up: demi-pointe, full pointe, demi-pointe flat. Tendu, turn in, turn out, and close. The girls feel their way into their bodies, and I watch. Sometimes a student needs guiding into her dancer's posture. I notice Kira wears a new leotard, and Maegyn has piled her long blond hair high on her head, a bow fastened against it at a jaunty angle. In the class before hers, another blond, younger, emulates Maegyn's look with a bow of her own, the neat bun taught to her by the girl she admires. I remember these gestures, the allure of those older students, the allure of a future filled with peachy-pink satin shoes and newly sewn ribbons.

One of the joys of being a ballet teacher is the moment when a student learns to rise on pointe, one of ballet's rites of passage, the change from a little girl's dancing to the work of becoming a ballerina. We begin pointe work with two hands on the barre. Learning to dance correctly sur les pointes is one of the most important aspects of a young dancer's training. There can be no shortcuts. It's slow and methodical work. Each dancer's eyes are wide and twinkling as she adjusts her body to hold herself up on her shoes for the first time. There is nothing quite like feeling the full length of the leg while balancing on pointe. She is taller, statelier, maybe even more beautiful than just a moment before.

Later will come blisters from too-hard shoes or too-soft ones, from overwork and not enough care. There will be foot baths with Epsom salts, hundreds of Band-Aids for heels and toes. The feet will cramp and ache. Shoes will cost a small fortune and never last long enough. But that is later.

For now, there is a sense of light, a sense of accomplishment, a sense that the future brings more dancing, balancing in retiré or arabesque, like the pictures in ballet books or New York City Ballet mailers. In pointe class, Kira works to hold her turnout as she balances in first position and slowly lowers her body. She presses her inner thighs, as if the insides of her legs are being glued together. When she starts to feel it, when it starts to look correct, her shy smile betrays the pleasure of accomplishment.

When someone thinks of classical ballet, it's probably not West Virginia that comes to mind. It goes against type. Morgantown, a city of about thirty thousand residents and thirty thousand more college students, has at least ten dance studios. The state of West Virginia sponsors a yearly dance festival for young dancers, one of the few of its kind. The state's first bachelor's degree in dance was offered well after the new millennium began. At best, we're a state full of contradictions.

West Virginia was my family's home, but most members have moved away or passed on. I came back to the state of my ancestors and fell into teaching ballet as I wrote about it. For whatever reason, this trajectory feels very West Virginian. Many people return to this state after retiring. Ours is an old population, in old mountains, where old ways sometimes are still the current ways, for better and sometimes for worse. I didn't come here to retire, of course. I shifted into a new self, one divided more equally between dancing and writing. Instead of trying to let go of one identity and take on the other, they converged. I can't put my finger on why it seems important that I'm teaching ballet in West Virginia. But it does. Could this have happened in any other place? Potentially. But it didn't.

Many people want to tell me "everything happens for a reason," when I talk about how I was a dancer and now am a dance teacher and writer. I hate the phrase. I feel that most things that happen are beyond reason. They just happen. To say that everything happens for a reason takes away my agency. I didn't spontaneously become a writer because I couldn't dance anymore. I worked hard over years to learn the craft of writing. I didn't start my writing by scribbling about dancing. That came later, as I found a capacity to reflect on my experiences. Giving myself time and space helped. What my dancing and my writing would have in common is my fierce devotion to each. Always determined, I kept at both even when it didn't seem like I'd be any good at either.

"If you knew you were going to have rheumatoid arthritis, would you still have become a dancer?" I can't say how many times I've heard this question or a version of it. As corny as it is to say, I am made from dance. Even in my after-stage life, my prior training and identity informs everything I do. I'm disciplined because I was a dancer; I deal with disappointment better because of that experience.

And occasionally I accept success with a dancer's quiet grace. That kind of delicacy continues to be a work in progress, like technique in daily dance class.

The joys and rewards of teaching ballet have been small, simple gifts that have added up over time into a vocation that, like my own dancing, has come to define my life. In the studio, working with my ballet students, I become my better self. I'm not interested in my own gain; I am wholly invested in the dancer before me. How can I help her?

I hope I teach my young dancers more than how to turn out or have lovely tendus. Dancing is an art, and it's the sense of artistry I hope to pass. I know that part of what made me want to be a ballerina was that ballet was beautiful to watch. In ballet, in those moments when you feel in possession of your body, there is the fleeting essence of something rare and imbued with meaning. Beauty becomes more feeling and less a look. The audience doesn't necessarily know all the technical feats a dancer may show on the stage. But the audience is discerning in the way it watches. To please her audience, a dancer must do more than execute steps. Technique must be there, but there is also that *je ne sais quoi*. When a dancer hits a perfect fifth, the audience thinks, *clean*. When her head and arms arrange just so, it pleases the eye. *Polished*. There's a difference, and we pay attention. There is more to learn from dancing than the dancing itself.

Alex has legs for days and eyes so blue and large they seem nearly impossible. When I first met her, her dancing was shy, her arms never fully used, and so one of the first things I vowed to work with her on was port de bras. The use of the arms and carriage of the upper body had once been a challenge for me, but later, after finding the right teachers, my own port de bras became a hallmark, not a blemish. I knew firsthand that the transformation could happen with work and care.

It is clear to me that Alex, like my younger dancers, loves to dance. With some students, a teacher can feel the desire. Others will have talent but won't always commit. It's okay, of course. No one should force a student to become a dancer. Sometimes a ballet student will find her passion elsewhere, and I try to remember that this, too, is a cause for celebration. We should all learn to find and cultivate our passions, and if ballet isn't one of them, there's no use forcing it. There's too much work. But for some ballet students, this desire to transform through movement will be a palpable feeling a teacher will detect from the student.

Alex adores adagio; she loves slow movement, she works on her extension, and she wants to elongate each movement as she achieves it. She has convinced herself she can't turn, but I see all the elements of good turning in her—if she can get over her own misgivings about pirouettes. She can jump, too, but she doesn't like allegro the way she does her adagio.

Not long ago, Alex would often get lost in a room full of dancers. She's a quiet, thoughtful girl, and sometimes her dancing can be characterized the same way. If you really look at Alex, she is stunningly beautiful: pale, smooth skin, honey-brown hair and those large, bluer than blue eyes. She looks the way that most people imagine ballet dancers look. Alex doesn't understand just how pretty she is. She's not one for makeup, and her dress in and out of the studio is simple and unadorned, which I suppose could make her seem plain to some but makes her elegant in an uncomplicated way. She's not assertive in traditional ways, but serene, like a character in a Jane Austen novel.

This serenity, in contemporary society, even in the ballet studio, is easy to overlook. I suppose that we tend toward firecrackers, toward *wow*, conditioned to look at tricks. *Look ma, no hands!* So often dance has become showy, aware and celebratory of that showiness. Reality TV is somewhat to blame and competitions, too. A quiet dancer, like a good poem, can be stunning and little noticed. A quiet dancer learns to inhabit the moment, but the entertainment-focused audience tends toward the flashy choreography, even when it is devoid of feeling.

In class, there's Alex, almost never absent, with her calm, imperturbable countenance—yes, countenance, as old-fashioned a word as it is. She has an untamped desire to dance, as though she's been backlit with ambition. To help her, we begin with those pesky pirouettes. I threaten to throw myself on the ground and hold her supporting leg up in relevé so she must continue to turn. She knows I'm just crazy enough that I might do it.

When I went to American Ballet Theatre, I was looking for some validation that I still belonged in the dancing world. I needed assurance that rheumatoid arthritis hadn't permanently severed the bond. What happened over three intense trips to the studios at 890 Broadway, New York City, transformed my relationship to ballet. I hadn't expected that.

No longer searching for proof of belonging, I let myself back into that world by tunneling through ballet's pedagogy. From this new cocoon I emerged more as a teacher, embracing my art through the desire to pass it to others. Maybe this was always the reason I wanted to attend ABT training; I just didn't recognize the pull. A dancer's most intimate relationship to ballet comes from the love a teacher imparts in every port de bras and carefully constructed combination. These gestures became my relearned mother tongue, expression distilled to its purest physical form.

At ABT, in Studio Nine where I attended most of my training, the mirrors are not attached to the walls. Instead, the length of mirror is set into a wood scaffolding on casters so the mirrors can be rolled about the studio. The dancers might be permitted to look, or the mirrors can be rolled way and the dancers cannot watch themselves. In many ways, my journey back to the studio has been much like those mirrors. I have looked back at the dancer I once was. Now, maneuvering without my reflection, I have to rely on what's already inside me. This process of turning what I know inside out in order to share it feels both exhilarating and terrifying. In earning each certificate from ABT, the paper didn't signify to me simply proof of a teaching credential. The certificate also signified a desire I thought I'd lost. Now my connection to dancing—as a dancer, teacher, and writer—manifests itself in a space beyond fear, and it echoes my heartbeat, as if all my connections to dancing are tethered and living in harmony. I can't live in a world unconnected to ballet. Learning choreography, I felt the figure-eight patterns on the floor. In the same way my memory often loops circles around significant moments, it is up to me to puzzle out their significance. Perhaps this fierce desire to have dance threaded through my identity started very young. Perhaps there would be no way to pull this thread from my identity without unraveling the whole. Will there always be a part of me made from ballet? I hope so.

My orthopedic surgeon was a kind and skillful man of few words. Even in his steady and sure hands, having knee surgery wasn't easy. I had the surgery the last day of June 2009 and finished physical therapy in November of that year, right before Thanksgiving, though I've continued the exercises since then. Even now, I keep an exercise bike in my home like the ones at the center where I attended physical therapy, and I use it, if not daily then at least several days a week. I don't do a very strenuous workout, but it helps to keep my prosthesis working well. It has allowed me greater mobility, greater ability to do the things I want to do, like teaching ballet. When I think about this, I think of my name: Renée. French for "reborn."

While I enjoy teaching, not all of my students are easy. Some drop in to take class but don't truly appreciate that technique has to be built over time. For these students, the idea of dance entices more than the actual work of dancing. Or they've convinced themselves that they're far more talented or well-trained than they are. This approach used to anger me. Now, subdued, I tend to let these students learn on their own that one must let go of ego and work to become a dancer. Even then, success is not a given. In grade school, I remember teachers who used to fall back on the old cliché, "You can do anything you put your mind to." I knew better because of my experience in the studio. I could train every day and still not be a dancer.

And yet, training is vital. Very few dancers will have professional careers of any kind without serious training, even if they have some talent. I don't know the odds for sure, but one might have a better chance winning the lottery than having a dance career without years and years of serious training.

I have also observed that some students let the desire to dance morph into obsession, and this obsession can become ugly. In extreme cases, the student's obsession becomes their parents' obsession. Or maybe the parent's obsession becomes the student's.

Sometimes I think about Raymond Lukens and Franco De Vita from American Ballet Theatre. Both were adamant that ballet students need also to be trained on how to be good people. As Raymond would often say, "They're going to be people longer than they're going to be dancers." He insisted that they be taught kindness and courtesy. My own teachers were strict about the way we treated one another, too.

Over the years, I've found that the nastiest parents tend to be overly involved in their child's pursuits. These parents strike me as people who had some unrequited dream that they're trying to live out through their kids. They invest their own identity in the accomplishments of their children, that dream of "making it" in ballet, and they find the like-minded among other parents, creating little Mommy Mafias. It doesn't matter if it's a competition studio or non-profit center where students in the "company" pay for the right to perform. The sad truth is that some studios fail to provide equitable dance education, embracing a star system where students and parents vie for teacher attention and lay out large sums of money on private instruction preparing for costly competitions and competitive auditions for top schools. These studios will deny their star-student mentality all the way to their phony auditions and bogus placement classes, but that faux caste system is obvious. Those students must square off their arabesques, must hit retiré in pirouette, the same technique as the students in serious training schools elsewhere. Yet the caste system rules the local dance scene, and the parents, more than anyone, allow it, support it. The questions remain: Even if the local students make it out into the dancing world, will that dancing be filled with beauty? Or have they been wired for something else?

Opportunity tends to find me when I least expect it. It was early fall when the director of WVU's dance program sat down for a chat with me and suggested I join the corps in a piece he was staging for the dance program's annual concert. The idea was crazy. By that point, my body was the equivalent of a moth-eaten sweater. I'd had knee replacement surgery, but that didn't make me performance ready. In any rational sense, I was well past a performing career.

I said yes, even though performing again was beyond reasonable.

According to the director, the piece, *Standing Tall,* would not be technically difficult. In earlier stagings, it had used nondancers in the corps. The choreography was meant for a large, diverse cast. It was designed to be emotionally moving, and this made it "difficult"—it depicted the events of 9/11.

On September 11, 2001, I was also well past my career in dance. I lived in Columbus, Ohio, where I worked for my father's company in various roles, mostly directing marketing and advertising efforts. Ironically, I was supposed to fly to meet a client on 9/11, but my flight had been canceled. The Columbus airport was locked down as state police and National Guard spilled into the airport, escorting passengers like me out. At first, I panicked about the client meeting. Later I would be relieved that my flight had been canceled.

Like others that day, I started to worry. I had friends in New York City: a close friend of my brother's worked near the towers. Of course, friends of mine danced in New York companies. My mother's cousin split his time between New York and Europe. Not people I thought of every day, but my mind composed lists of those who might be in the city, wondering, are they okay?

One day, during rehearsal for the upcoming concert, the director challenged us to think back to our experiences on 9/11. There was an emotional quality to *Standing Tall* he felt was missing. It was only after rehearsal that I realized that most of the dancers I would be performing with had been in middle school when it happened. Not that those middle school students couldn't have a strong reaction, but it would be different from an adult's reaction. I remembered how I was supposed to fly to Boston, of all places, to the airport where the terrorists boarded the doomed flights. Had I gone, I probably would have been stranded in a strange city, reeling from the events, and then I'd have to fly home. Flying in the days and weeks after 9/11 would have been terrifying. Panic and fragmentation balled up inside me, waiting to be unleashed in simple, stark movements.

I have often wondered what the people who lost their lives in the tragedies of 9/11 would think of us, those of us not dead, living our lives, experiencing our triumphs and our shortcomings and our setbacks. I wonder what they might have done differently in their own lives, had they known. But you can never know. Things happen beyond reason.

Standing Tall was set to Bach, *Air on the G String*, music many might not know by name but would probably recognize if they heard it. It is calm, almost meditative, not a piece one would expect to be associated with 9/11. The choreography consisted of moments when individual cast members moved in different directions, walking or running, alone or in groups. At times the whole cast danced as one, then fragmented again. I remembered figure eights.

Standing Tall tested my range because the vocabulary—the steps—were all modern technique. I never considered myself much of a modern dancer, although I'd had many years of study as part of my development as a ballet dancer. To add to my unease, the studio was filled with younger dancers—some current or recent ballet students I had taught. I felt old and awkward among them, and not just because I was dancing with one fake knee.

My complicated feelings toward this performance also
stemmed from the past. I didn't know that my last performance as a ballet dancer was my last. Some dancers prepare
for retirement. I was literally performing pirouettes and
grands jétés one day and swelling in my joints another.
Rehearsals took their toll as twinges reminded me my
physical body had changed. To do even the simplest movements, I needed an extensive warm-up. So I arrived early
to each rehearsal to do pliés and tendus, to stretch, to align
my body, to practice floor work. Ballet doesn't use the floor
the way modern technique does. In *Standing Tall* we rolled,
we kneeled; we swept our bodies across the floor's plane. In
order to do this with my surgery scar and new knee, I had
to invest in knee pads. My middle, gone soft, required daily
crunches and other abdominal exercises. My inner thighs,
flabby with disuse, required tendus, degagés, grands battements à la seconde—all the regimens of my youth.

Still, I felt fat and sluggish. But I was steadfast. When I
was sore and tired from rehearsing, when I had RA flares
from pushing myself too hard, I remembered that so few
of us get a do-over, a second chance, another opportunity.
Blessings often come soaked in sweat and sometimes with
bruises, purples that yellow and eventually heal back to flesh.

I'd once read that those who suffer from rheumatoid arthritis
tend to have a 30 percent shorter lifespan than those who
don't have the disease. I don't remember where I'd read this
or if the source was reputable. What I do remember is thinking that my RA might shorten my life, and there would be
no way of getting my time back. Time has become the most
important resource to me. As such, I've ceased to teach in
independent studios that treat me as anything less than
a professional. No Mommy Mafias. In fact, if I don't feel

respected for my teaching, I find other places to bring my skills. I have found studios not only where I feel valued but where I've valued others. One of my new colleagues, Cara, went to the American Ballet Theatre for teacher training, and I helped her write a grant to the West Virginia Commission on the Arts to fund it. I went with Cara to New York for the training, sharing a room, meals, and nightly study sessions together. The only thing we didn't do together was the exam. Cara would get her own thick envelope, her own certificate.

My RA shapes me but doesn't define me, and because of my struggles I find more positive outlets for what I do with my dancing. I work to be as supportive of other teachers as they are toward me. They are not just my colleagues but my friends. We share the joy of ballet through teaching. We share in the success of our students' acceptances to summer programs: Kira and Meghan to American Ballet Theatre, Emily to Ballet Met and Milwaukee Ballet, Maegyn to Gelsey Kirkland Academy, Maddie on full scholarship to the Governor's School for the Arts. All this in just over two years of working together. Teaching ballet takes time and hard work, but these successes in both professional friendships and student accomplishments are signs that I'm pursuing a better path. No longer do I think of the precious time that RA might take away; I know that I'm using my time and talents wisely. Time is no longer an hourglass running out of sand.

There is exactly one person who has seen me come full circle as a performer: my brother, Nate. He watched my performances when I was younger, when my dancing was full of promise and technical ability. And, in the dreary February weather, he drove from Dublin, Ohio, to Morgantown, West Virginia, to see me return to the stage.

I told him not to expect too much; it wouldn't be the same as before.

"It won't be the same as watching you use a walker to get around, either," he said.

It's good to remember that the body, even in disrepair, is a wonder, and that healing happens in ways we might never understand.

The day of the performance, the dressing rooms were buzzing with chatter, and I was happy that, as a faculty member, I had a room to myself. It wasn't that I felt I was better than the student dancers, but there was a different energy among those dancers than what I felt. For the most part, their preperformance routine was jubilant, full of laughter. Mine was quiet, and I think my stoicism might have been misinterpreted. It may have come off as stony, judgmental. I might have seemed ungrateful for the performing opportunity. Emotions tend to gather inside me, released only by the hot stage light and music. Before performance, I'm contemplative, almost meditative. It's as if all my energy is being stored, to be channeled into the moment of dancing.

During the preparations for our Saturday matinee, there was a knock on my dressing room door. It was Maureen, the director's wife, a former Paul Taylor dancer with an easy way about her. Her soft blond hair framed her face but would be swept back for performance. She'd forgotten to pack moisturizer in her stage makeup kit. "Can I borrow some?" she asked.

This reminded me the most of my past performing days, where things were routinely shared and swapped. I welcomed her in, searched my makeup kit for moisturizer. I'd been using some that also filled in fine lines, and I offered it to her with the explanation, "It's all I've got." She dabbed a little bit from the jar on her finger, sampled its smooth, silky texture.

"It's not what I expected," she said after patting it under her eye. "But it's nice." She smiled and confessed to forgetting a few other items at home. With her two young kids, I couldn't imagine trying to get ready for performance. I pulled out other items from my kit, and she tried this and that. We talked about how hungry we got after performance, craving steaks. I confessed that my skin wasn't used to the heavy makeup anymore.

Before she left, Maureen said, "I love to watch you in *Standing Tall*. You dance with so much emotion."

After all the years of not dancing, perhaps emotion is all I have left. Maureen's words pierced me, and I wanted to burst or break. Instead, I gathered it in. I don't even remember what I said in return, but I'm sure it was polite and placid and that I resumed warming my body for what I knew was ahead.

Lindsay's hair is so fair it looks like it could have been spun from a brick of gold. She has the longest eyelashes I've ever seen. By the last semester I worked with her, she'd become a black-leotard-and-pink-tights kind of dancer, her hair pulled back into a classic knot. The metamorphosis wasn't just in her appearance but in her technique. When Lindsay joined the WVU dance program, she clearly had an "it" factor when it came to the stage. She was the kind of performer who danced with unbridled emotion. Naturally dramatic, she put adjectives into motion: fierce, composed, strong, confused, thoughtful, grief-stricken, or elated. Music didn't provide mood for Lindsay's dancing but enhanced her movement.

When I first met Lindsay, her background had not involved much ballet. Many university students ended up in my class not because they loved classical ballet but because they saw ballet technique as a way to become stronger dancers in other forms—modern and jazz. I think, like Lindsay, these students saw that I invested in hard workers regardless of their favorite style.

By the time Lindsay graduated, she had earned a solo in my ballet *Quiet Heart*. I remember when I called her after auditions to offer her the role. Excitement bubbled up, though she tried to keep her voice even. I knew that she would commit herself to the piece. Lindsay opened it, dancing not to music but spoken word. This would be a challenge, because music gives strong sonic cues to the movement. Still, Lindsay never danced with anything less than her whole self. Her dancing became expression at its most basic and most pure.

Some days my hands are swollen, my knees hot with fluid and it hurts to walk, let alone dance. My feet like sausages in tight casing. While I often talk about the trajectory from writer to dance teacher, it feels like that metamorphosis is more complicated. The three components—RA, writing, and dancing—weave into who I am. As RA irrevocably changed my body from that of a dancer, I learned more about my body and how it did and didn't work.

Anything forced will end up changing the way muscles work, and the way muscles work changes the way they look. Dancers have long lean muscles, turned out and elongated, fashioned from the way they train. Compare the muscles of a dancer to the compact, punchy, explosive ones of a gymnast. I don't know a lot about gymnastic training, but the kinds of tumbling passages gymnasts execute on the floor or on the balance beam require a different musculature than a dancer pressing through her muscles to alight on pointe. My awareness of these differences is informed by the way my own body changed through dealing with my disease—a kind of cursed blessing, or perhaps a blessed curse.

It's hard to make sense of it all, even to me, even as I write about it. Maybe the capacity to teach is already in those of us who end up in the profession. Maybe all the years of wanting to understand my technique, of trying to absorb everything I could from my teachers, were stored in some special place in my brain waiting to be tapped. Maybe the voice of my dancing self searches the page for a way to describe the act rather than be completely silenced. My body quieted, I receive the lessons again.

Balmy for a February night in Morgantown, the West Virginia University Dance Program's *Dance Now!* concert had been delayed twice by a malfunctioning fire alarm, and the entire crowd had been ushered out and back in each time. The uncharacteristically warm weather worked in our favor, as the lobby was full while the house prepared for the late start. I sold *Dance Now!* T-shirts in the lobby, one of many glamorous duties as a part-time, adjunct ballet instructor in a university dance program. Various people came by to say hello as I manned the table. Several former students came up to buy shirts and give hugs. Parents stopped to peruse the silent auction, buy merchandise for their kids, and, often, offer a compliment about my classes.

People often use events like this performance to chat me up about summer programs and other performances, and what Pittsburgh Ballet Theater would perform in the University Arts Series. Since I have knowledge and contacts, I get asked for opinions on these and other dance-related topics. At this show, as I sold T-shirts, the parent of one of my current students came up with a friend whose son took dance classes. This friend simply wanted advice and insight into summer programs where her son had gained acceptance, and I could provide some outside opinions for her. Then, things progressed in slow motion. From across the lobby, a woman with cropped brown hair and a frigid stare saw this introduction. She made a beeline for the table, eyes wide with rage. As the new parent extended her hand toward mine, she was immediately clutched by both shoulders, and turned, like a disobedient child. The woman with cropped dark hair led the other woman away from my table. My student's parent stood a moment as her jaw dropped. My hands dropped to the table, and I'm sure my expression had sagged into bewilderment. My husband, a level-headed CPA who happened to be standing next to the table, looked at me as if I'd been slapped.

The woman with cropped brown hair happened to be the president of the board of the local not-for-profit dance studio where I had once taught years ago. Don of the Mommy Mafia, she was letting me know how she felt about the fact that I dared to leave. I wonder if she realizes the toxic affect her actions—whether toward me or toward others—have on her organization and all the parents and students within it? This surreal moment in the foyer served as a reminder that I had, in fact, made a wise decision. I always hope that their approach might change, if for no other reason than for the sake of the dancing, which should always remain full of beauty.

My last performance of *Standing Tall* was a matinee. Afterward I ate a hamburger with my brother, Nate, at the local pub. The burger was thick, juicy, and marinated in teriyaki, blending traditional and unconventional flavors. Most people probably think dancers adhere to strict diets. After performing, I always needed to eat large, and after *Standing Tall* I was as famished as I remember being after *Nutcracker* or *Sleeping Beauty* or *Cinderella*. Nate and I ordered oatmeal stouts and toasted my return to the stage.

What we didn't talk about was that my return might be another exit. I don't know how much performing I have left in me. Maybe cameos and character roles. Every *Nutcracker* needs a grandmother, some a "tipsy granny" character, more acting than dancing. While I don't talk about *Standing Tall* as my ultimate curtain call, in many ways it fills this void. Yet there's always a chance for another twirl on stage.

Perhaps I don't think about performing so much because I'm focused more on teaching and writing. My preoccupations are less about the roles I'll be in and more about what I have to say and pass on. Teaching is always a kind of performance, and I plan and practice my classes for this role I play.

However, I will never forget that afternoon of burgers and beer. My brother made it a prerogative to see me back on the stage. As we ate, we laughed about the younger version of me, watching TV in the splits. My hands caressed the pint glass; the stout was cold and stiff, just what I needed. My return had been witnessed. Sharing it meant that I would never be alone in my memories of dancing.

"Can you meet me?" Jessica says. "I need to talk to you."

Jessica, civil engineering student at WVU, is also pursuing a dance minor. With nearly a 4.0 grade point average, Jessica's future in engineering, where women are still a scarce commodity, looks bright. But on the last day of winter break I receive her call.

At a coffee shop off campus, I sit for three hours with Jessica. Her brown eyes light up with determination. She's not yet ready to be done with dancing but has only two semesters left in school. Can she still make it in a professional company?

As her instructor, the moment fills me with ache. Can she make it? Technically, yes. But everything will be stacked against her. She'll be competing against younger dancers who've trained more. They will come from prominent dance schools. Even the elite college dance programs struggle to place dancers in professional companies. She will have to earn her stripes in trainee programs, where her competition will include teenagers still in or fresh from high school. She will need to train daily, even with her full academic load. This will include augmenting her university technique classes with other classes in the community, Pilates, whatever she can manage.

Faced with these odds, nearly all other students would give up, but Jessica begins taking 7 a.m. Pilates daily at the student rec center. She audits every advanced dance class offered—modern, jazz, ballet. She improves.

That summer Jessica figures out how she can work as an intern at an engineering firm in Manassas, Virginia, as well as participate in the summer intensive at Manassas Ballet. She works from 7 a.m. to 3 p.m. for the engineering firm, and then dances from 4 p.m. to 9 p.m., Monday through Friday.

I meet with Jessica again when she returns from her summer in Virginia. Her skin nearly glows. "I have a trainee contract," she says. "In Manassas. After I graduate."

So many won't make it, but sometimes, if you're lucky, you cross paths with a Jessica. With those students, odds don't matter. Desire fuels passion, and it's this potent mixture that allows certain people to overcome circumstance. That's what Jessica reminds me. And while I'm not responsible for her success, I hope that in some small way, I've helped her. When I close my eyes, I can see her perfectly halved chaînés, tight circles across the studio, somehow both fierce and delicate.

There is no way for me to undo what rheumatoid arthritis has done. I will never feel my body quite like I did when I was a dancer. When I write about dancing, there is a sense of grief that's underneath it, pushing me to try to capture on the page what I have lost. Even when the writing doesn't reflect grief, it's the catalyst. And yet, RA has never fully taken ballet from me, even in physical form. Sometimes, when I demonstrate first arabesque or some other position to my students, I see shades of the dancer I'd once been. She is lurking inside me, and sometimes in the studio my body feels a bit of what it did once when my days were made of dancing.

I write of dancing as if composing a love letter. This love is pure and sometimes cruel, creating moments of sublime peace and others of despair. All true love tends to wrap itself in these contradictions. My love letters to dance, I hope, lift me up from my disease and into the realm where imagination and experience blend together in complicated pas de deux. Loops made of fierce and delicate turns, into waiting arms, into lifts and balances.

When I lay my head on my pillow each night, eyes closed, there is dance. Tomorrow I wake and in some way am connected to dance. There will always be pliés and tendus, as there will also be students and friends. Strains of music, humid studios, ambition and light. And blank pages. I am here shaping those tales, an afterglow, after stage, in the soft light of dusk in the Mountain State.

Six Impossible Things Before Breakfast

ONE

A White Queen lives in the hillsides outside Morgantown, West Virginia. Her skin smooth, pale. Her hair coiled, pinned, the color of spun gold. Tall, statuesque even, long limbed.

When she's not a queen, she's an honors student.

TWO

West Virginia: where I came to heal. Where my people are from.

I never thought I'd be a ballet teacher. I never thought that if I were to become a ballet teacher that I would teach dance in Morgantown, West Virginia. And definitely not one who would train a White Queen. I don't just mean a student who gets a role in a community ballet production, who suffers the slings and arrows of strange alliances and competing studio politics. I don't just mean a student who gets invited to schools in big, faraway cities. The White Queen of whom I speak is more than just a white queen.

When I train a student, some of what comes out is unique to her. And some is what's been passed to me, and those who taught me, and those who trained those who taught me, like the looking glass always reflecting backward, until we reach the actual royal courts where the stylish Catherine de Medici wed a Bourbon king of France. She brought much with her from Italy, including her balleti master and the fledgling form of dance. The French ended up calling the new form of dance *ballet* and were mad for it.

And so the art traveled to Denmark, England, and Russia, where it took its various accents until it crossed an ocean to New York City. From there, it spread across the wide continent, even to the nooks and valleys where I now live. Of course, I didn't bring ballet here, just the technique of it picked up from teachers in South Florida and Northern Michigan and Milwaukee and New York. I brought their particular sautés and port de bras and pirouettes. Their pithy sayings and hard-and-fast rules.

I never set out to teach ballet. Maybe it found me. When it did, I studied pedagogy, curated libraries of books, DVDs, music, workshops, certifications. Articulation in words and in movement. I needed to know how everything worked, relearn what my own body once knew. Here, at the barre, I give plié, tendu, fondu, grand battement in a dialect made my own.

THREE

Sophisticated, elegant, fair. Adjectives jump to their feet in service to the White Queen. Her deep concentration, meticulous technique, keeps her preoccupied. She is wholly unaware of her beauty, which, I suppose, is the way of the true royal.

In the Alice books, the White Queen lives in Wonderland, or Through the Looking Glass. Maybe she really believed six impossible things before breakfast. Then tea and biscuits.

FOUR

My White Queen does not miss anything—not class, not corrections, and never the chance to perform. She adores grace in all its forms. She loves épaulement, épaulé, all the shouldered movements, all the texture and drama. Renaissance painters would clamor for her simple croisée devant, cheek poised to be kissed. Defiant écarté, as if looking in a pocket mirror high above her head.

My younger self, buried under a broken body and graying bun, still understands. I remember performance as doing the thing in front of others for the push and thrill, that rush of *will I get it just right*? Different high-stakes perfection than the mirror and teacher and other pupils.

I taught the White Queen her pirouettes. She swore she'd never be a turner. I once believed the same—*not a turner*—until one day I was.

FIVE

A long dormant past awoke, a Sleeping Beauty, not of body but of mind and soul. I remember a different White Queen attacking her dégagé at the barre. Later it will become allegro steps, jumps. Assemblé. Glissade. Light. Quick. Fast. Jumping is strength tempered by grace, beauty fortified with speed.

When I watch, I almost remember it in my own body, like searching for the word on the tip of the tongue. But the word never comes, is never uttered. The White Queen moves silently over the floor in brisk, fleeting steps.

SIX

When the White Queen inevitably relinquishes her crown, her platter tutu, hangs her well-worn slippers, it will still be my job to give exercises at the barre and center. It will still be my job to usher hopefuls through the ritual that is pointe work. Fresh new faces, eager, my charges for a few hours, as if this is how the princess and the duchess find themselves royal. Sometimes it is just technique and work and sweat and tears.

Among them, perhaps, not a White Queen but a Red. I only have clues. *Divide a loaf by a knife: what's the answer to that?* It's a language of queens, and ballet their movement. All the mysteries to be unlocked. Perhaps only a queen truly knows. I was once enveloped in white.

Acknowledgments

IT'S IMPOSSIBLE to thank all the people I should, yet certainly this book owes all the support from my parents, Connie and Nick Nicholson, who sustained many years of dance instruction, as well as my husband, Matt Bauman, for supporting my writing. With gratitude to my friends Dominique Bruno Mick and Stacey Culp, who support and inspire me in equal parts. Thanks to John Hoppenthaler, my longtime friend and writing mentor, the one who always said I should write a book about ballet.

Three very important people in this book died before it was published. In loving memory of my brother, Nate Nicholson, and the dancers Peter Franklin-White and Laurie Picinich-Byrd.

A special thank-you to Penn State Altoona for its support of my writing as the 2011 emerging writer-in-residence. Many of the essays in this book were composed and revised during my time there. Particular thank-you to Erin Murphy for all her advice and friendship.

A special thank-you to Raymond Lukens and Franco De Vita of American Ballet Theatre and the ABT National Training Curriculum program. Also, thank you to the faculty and staff of the Professional Certificate in Narrative Medicine at Columbia University. Both programs changed me for the better as an artist, writer, teacher, and person.

To all of my colleagues in the Eberly College of Arts and Sciences and specifically in the programs in Multi- and Interdisciplinary Studies and Regents Bachelor of Arts at West Virginia University, thanks for your support. To all of my students of ballet, writing, and other pursuits, it's always been a privilege to be a part of your development, and you often inspire the writing itself. A special thanks to Keegan Lester, once a student and now a dear friend and talented writer himself, and to Evan Widders, my former chair and always friend.

A special thank-you to all my dance teachers. I was not always the easiest student. A note about using names of people and schools: in some cases, I opted not to use formal names in order to be respectful, and compressed similar experiences to keep from being repetitive.

There are too many writers to name who have had a profound influence on me, but Renée D'Aoust, the dancer and writer, showed me so much that was possible between the two worlds. Thanks to her and all the writers who had a hand in guiding me, and to Janet Nurkiewicz for reading the early versions. Special thanks to Carl Gray, Monika Holbein, Dana Huebert-Lima, Allison Lastinger, Clay Marsh, Betsy Pyle, Rosanna Sikora, Rondalyn Whitney, and all the others who have helped me see the important connections between health and writing.

And, finally, thanks to my weekly lunches with my favorite curmudgeonly reader/editor for the regular writing talk, inspiration, fun, and occasional venting that keeps me going as a writer.

Notes

10 "I was no more than eleven . . ." Gelsey Kirkland, *Dancing on My Grave* (New York: Berkley Books, 1992), 30.

12 "First comes the sweat . . ." Bernard Taper, *Balanchine: A Biography* (1974, repr. Berkeley, CA: University of California Press, 1996), 4.

13 "The mirror is not you . . ." Margaret Fuhrer, "The Best Balanchine Quotes in Honor of Mr. B's Birthday," *Dance Spirit*, January 22, 1998.

14 "The myth was that because you were black . . ." "Arthur Mitchell," Kennedy Center, accessed August 14, 2020, https://www.kennedy-center.org/artists/m /ma-mn/arthur-mitchell/.

22 "The ballet is a purely female thing . . ." Balanchine quoted in Curt Sachs, *World History of Dance* (New York: W. W. Norton, 1937), 48.

23 **"Dancing is like bank robbery . . ."** Tharp quoted in Deborah Jowitt, "Twyla Tharp," *The Bulletin*, January 1976.

23 **"All we actually have is our body . . ."** Allegra Kent, *Once a Dancer: An Autobiography* (New York: St. Martin's Press, 1998).